Vital Leglocks

65 leglocks for jujitsu, judo, sambo and mixed martial arts

D1069443

Vital Leglocks

65 leglocks for jujitsu, judo, sambo and mixed martial arts

By Steve Scott

 Turtle Press   Santa Fe

JESSAMINE COUNTY PUBLIC LIBRARY
600 South Main Street
Nicholasville, KY 40356
(859) 885-3523

VITAL LEGLOCKS Copyright © 2007 Steve Scott. All rights reserved. Printed in the United States of America. No part of this book may be reproduced without written permission except in the case of brief quotations embodied in articles or reviews. For information, address Turtle Press, PO Box 34010, Santa Fe NM 87594-4010.

To contact the author or to order additional copies of this book:
call 1-800-778-8785 or visit www.TurtlePress.com

ISBN 978-1-880336-96-0
LCCN 2007034421
Printed in the United States of America

10 9 8 7 6 5 4 3 2

Warning-Disclaimer

This book is designed to provide information on specific skills used in the sport of sambo, also known as sombo. It is not the purpose of this book to reprint all the information that is otherwise available to the author, publisher, printer or distributors, but instead to compliment, amplify and supplement other texts. You are urged to read all available material, learn as much as you wish about the subjects covered in this book and tailor the information to your individual needs. Anyone practicing the skills presented in this book should be physically capable to do so and have the permission of a licensed physician before participating in this activity or any physical activity.

Every effort has been made to make this book as complete and accurate as possible. However, there may be mistakes, both typographical and in content. Therefore, this text should be used only as a general guide and not the ultimate source of information on the subjects presented here in this book on sambo or any skill or subject. The purpose of this book is to provide information and entertain. The author, publisher, printer and distributors shall neither have liability nor responsibility to any person or entity with respect to loss or damages caused, or alleged to have been caused, directly or indirectly, by the information contained in this book.

Library of Congress Cataloguing in Publication Data

Scott, Steve, 1952-
  Vital leglocks : 65 leglocks for jujitsu, judo, sambo and mixed martial arts / by Steve Scott.
    p. cm.
  ISBN 978-1-880336-96-0
  1. Hand-to-hand fighting, Oriental. 2. Wrestling. 3. Mixed martial arts. I. Title.
  GV1112.S453 2007
  796.815--dc22
                              2007034421

DEC 1 3 2010

3 2530 60703 0507

Acknowledgements

Thanks to the following people for appearing in the photos used in this book: John Saylor, Bill West, Shawn Watson, Chris Heckadon, Bryan Potter, Eric Millsap, Bob Rittman, Jarrod Fobes, Josh Henges, Bret Holder, Travis Oliphant, Ed Rogers, Will Cook, Rusty Frederick, Kirt Yoder, John Zabel, Ben Goehrung, Kyle Meredith, Chris Vanderberg, Chris Bartley, Trevor Finch, Drew Hills, Sean Wheelock, Frederic Leyd, Greg Fetters, Chance Powers, Bill Brown, Jim Fisher, Brian Lepic, John Begley and Vince Vitatoe. Photos taken at Welcome Mat, Kansas City, Missouri, Bill Brown's Karate, Kearney, Missouri and the Barn of Truth, Perrysville, Ohio. Photography by Steve Scott, Bill West, Jamie Scott, Eric Millsap and Andy Fonseca.

Contents

INTRODUCTION

Without a doubt, the legs and hips are the strongest part of the human body, and to attack and ultimately apply a submission technique on this part of the body takes a lot of guts, determination and skill.

From my experience, there are people out there who are leglock specialists. These are the guys who are the risk-takers and seemingly enjoy the challenge of matching their skills against an opponent's strongest body part. Even the ankle lock and toehold specialists have to contend with manipulating an opponent's lower body to be able to effectively control the ankle and gain the advantage.

This book is for these leglock specialists, but it's just as much for anyone who wants to study effective and practical lower body submissions in a systematic way. Make no mistake about it; this book isn't the final answer on the art and science of leglocks. It's my personal point of view on the subject based on my background as an athlete, coach and student of the art and science of manipulating the human body. However, I have attempted to provide a comprehensive study of leglocks and realistic ways to apply them on an unwilling opponent.

Many years ago, my friend Jim Martin impressed upon me the importance of following the KISS principle as it related to learning and doing skills on the mat. As many of you know, KISS is the acronym for "Keep It Simple Stupid." Jim (or I) never mean to imply that keeping things simple is the same as being stupid, but it does mean that the simpler things are, the better they seem to work. This is certainly the case for leglocks. My approach to lower body submissions (and the primary focus of this book) is to go for the high percentage moves. You only have a few seconds for your window of opportunity to set up any submission technique, and this is especially true for leglocks. While there are some very interesting, complex, technical applications of leglocks that require several steps to execute, my goal is to focus in on the skills that are fundamentally sound, can be applied from a variety of situations and have a high ratio of success. I prefer the simpler, high-percentage moves, and I think most people are like me in this regard. Master skills you know you can rely on and be able to work them from a variety of positions and situations.

9

For this reason, I have tried to emphasize the joint locks directed at the ankle and foot in this book. The section that includes the ankle locks, toeholds and heel hooks is larger than the other sections for good reason. From my experience in sambo, the submission techniques directed against the ankle and feet have a higher ratio of success than those directed at the leg and knee. An ankle is easier to bend or twist than a leg or knee. Also, it seems that the further a body part is away from the head, the harder it is for your opponent to defend. For whatever reason, the ankle locks, toeholds and heel hooks seem to work more consistently than other leglocks, but by saying this, I don't mean to dissuade you from developing good skills at leg or knee locks. Really, it's a personal preference of mine and I encourage you to experiment with a variety of leg and ankle locks in your training to see what works best for you.

Grapplers in any style of sport combat have a natural tendency to protect the upper body first, and then realize the lower body is vulnerable. Most people tend to use their lower extremities to propel and balance themselves by jumping, running, standing, squatting or placing themselves in other similar positions. Rarely, unless you've trained to think this way, do you think of your feet and legs as you would your hands and arms. Grapplers who are trained to use every part of their bodies as tools to manipulate an opponent tend to think of their feet and legs in the same way as their hands and arms. If you think of your lower body in this way, you will be more aware of what (and where) your lower extremities are doing all the time and will be less likely to be vulnerable to having a leg or ankle lock placed on you.

Leglock specialists know that most opponents instinctively protect their upper bodies and tend to try to position themselves so they can get to their opponent's knees and ankles as fast as possible. For this reason, Section One of this book takes a serious look at the positions and situations found in lower body grappling. Good position is vital in every aspect of grappling and leg, ankle and hip locks are no different.

I've categorized lower body submissions into several primary groups, with each group focusing on a particular joint and method of manipulation. Section Two looks at ankle and foot locks, including heel hooks and toeholds. Section Three highlights locks against the knee, both straight and bent. Section Four examines hip locks, which in reality aren't "leglocks" but they are effective lower body submissions and in some cases, attacking an opponent's hip joint may involve attacking another joint in the leg or foot as well.

Good mechanics and fundamental technical skill are important in leglocks as in the study of any part of grappling. Realistically, there's a right way and a wrong way to perform a move, but once you've come to understand and be able to perform the fundamentally correct method of any technique in this book, take it to the next level and make that technique work for you. Mold it to fit your needs. Everybody's different. We all have different strength levels, tactics, height, weight, backgrounds, goals and motivation. If there is a move shown in this book that would work for you in a different way, don't hesitate to make the changes necessary to make it successful for you.

The photographs for this book were taken in the dojos and gyms where my athletes, colleagues and I train. The familiar refrain "Steve's got his camera out again!" was heard more often than not in the making of this book and I am deeply grateful to the athletes and coaches who helped me make it a reality. Their talent had much to do with this effort. I also want to thank Turtle Press and Cynthia Kim for the support they have shown me in the entire process of producing this book. My wife Becky offered much technical and editorial advice and helped make this book what it is.

My background is in sambo, jujitsu and judo, but I am also an admirer of the legitimate professional wrestlers who were the superstars of professional sports in the early 1900s in the United States. Great professional wrestlers like Frank Gotch and Farmer Burns (among others) were masters of submission holds, especially leglocks. Frank Gotch retired as the undefeated heavyweight champion of professional wrestling in 1913 and was known for his toehold. He forced many men to submit to the pain he inflicted on them from the hold he made famous. While the old-timers were truly masters of lower body submission holds, we have people today who are also highly skilled exponents of leg submissions such as Gene LeBell, John Saylor, Scott Sonnen and others. Men like these keep the art and science of leglocks alive and I hope this book adds to the body of practical knowledge and can be used as a reliable reference for years to come.

SAFETY WHEN DOING LEGLOCKS

It's been my experience that people tend to tap out from the pain of an ankle or knee lock a bit too late. This isn't the case in hip or lower back submissions, as the pain is pretty overwhelming in these situations. However, I've seen a lot of guys get torn ligaments or tendons in their knees because they didn't feel the pain of the lock soon enough and an injury took place. In sambo, it's considered a sign of submission when one wrestler taps or yells. Often, the natural thing to do when hurt is to yell, grunt or groan and it's for the wrestler's wellbeing that this rule is in effect.

When you practice lower body submissions or have them applied on you in a competitive situation, make sure to tap out or show an accepted sign of submission when the lock is fully applied and you know you have no chance of escaping. As with other submission techniques observe the common sense of the old saying; "When in doubt, tap out."

Additionally, I recommend that you warm and stretch your muscles and joints completely before practicing or doing lower body submissions. You're less likely to get injured (or tapped out) if you have a good, functional range of motion in your joints.

THE MAJOR TYPES OF LEGLOCKS

When we talk about leglocks, we're really talking about submission techniques aimed at the lower body. I classify lower body submissions into three major areas. They are:

- Ankle and Foot Locks
- Knee Locks
- Hip and Upper Leg Locks.

This book will focus in on these three areas of lower body submissions from a practical point of view. How and why a particular skill works will be presented because it's important for anyone reading this to not only know how a move works, but why it works. Each section of this book will present a variety of submission techniques that have been used by somebody somewhere to make somebody else tap out.

SECTION ONE:
Lower Body Grappling, Leg Wrestling, Position, Breakdowns and Set-ups

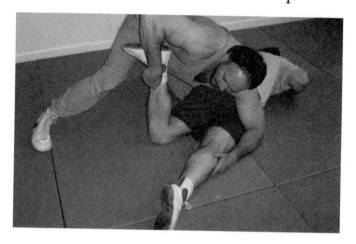

"Control your opponent and impose your will on him."
Steve Scott

Before you can get a leglock on your opponent, you have to control his body, especially his lower body from the hips down. The better you limit his movement by controlling his legs, hips and pretty much everything else about your opponent, the better you will be able to sink in a leglock. The art and science of attacking your opponent's hips, legs and ankles is often called "lower body grappling" or "leg wrestling." Sometimes, you can snatch an ankle lock or leglock from a scramble position where neither you nor your opponent have the advantage as far as position goes. But being able to get there first to apply the ankle lock before he does is the result of you being more alert to where you are in relation to your opponent. Suffice it to say that if you always try to be in the best position possible to control your opponent and apply a submission technique, you will have the tendency to be the first one to slap on a leglock when the opportunity presents itself.

If you've read my other books, you know that I am a firm believer in controlling the position. There's no luck to it at all. Position is being in the right place at the right time and putting your opponent in the wrong place (for him) every time. As said earlier, if you are a "position grappler" you will have a better sense of how your body should be in relation to your opponent, where you and your opponent are on the mat (mat space) and will be better able to take advantage of any opportunity that arises. Your opponent may simply make a mistake, but if you're not in the right place to take advantage of it, you will have missed your chance to capitalize on his mistake.

The greatest part of my experience in applying leglocks has been in sambo, but I have a sincere appreciation for the many toeholds, knee cranks and other lower body submission techniques that have come from the legitimate professional wrestling that has, unfortunately, faded into America's past. Because of this, I've tried to show a number of positions common to every form of submission grappling and wrestling practiced in this section. Good grappling, whether it's sambo, jujitsu, submission grappling or mixed martial arts, is moving from one position to another position to even another position and trying to control your opponent and ultimately make him give up to you.

Also shown are some common sense tips that are necessary for effective and reliable lower body submissions. This is the kind of information that separates an athlete who knows what he wants and how to get it from the athlete who wishes he had trained harder and smarter in the gym. Some of these tips may seem pretty obvious, but don't neglect them or take them for granted. They can be good friends to you when you need them!

Use Your Feet and Legs Like You Do Your Hands and Arms

Think of your feet as you do your hands and your legs as you do your arms. To be a good lower body grappler, you need to develop a keen ability to manipulate your opponent's body using your feet, legs and even your hips. In this photo, Travis is about to wrap his right foot in Rusty's right leg to counter Rusty's ankle lock.

Wrestler's Ride (Get His Back)

A good rule of thumb is to always try to get behind your opponent and don't allow him to get behind you. If he can't see you, you have a better chance of setting him up for a leglock or other submission technique. Notice how Chris "has his opponent's back" and is riding Bob. Chris is controlling Bob by staying slightly behind Bob's left hip and controlling Bob's hips and lower body. Chris stays on his toes as shown and constantly keeps close contact between his opponent's back and hip and his own chest. By staying on his toes, Chris is mobile and can move freely. He also makes sure to use his weight and body movement to limit Bob's movement. Whenever Bob moves, Chris exerts pressure to control where he goes. Chris can use this position as a good start to further work another position and gain more control over Bob's body. Chris uses Bob's hips and lower back as a point of contact from which he can swivel to any direction. Often, when going for leglocks, the top grappler will have to quickly turn to face his opponent's feet, so it's important to think of your opponent's hips and lower back as the point where you work from. If you're the grappler riding your opponent, you have a distinct and decided advantage and can work a lot of set-ups from this position.

The photo below shows how the top grappler can start from a wrestler's ride and spin around using the bottom man's lower back and hips as a fulcrum and go for lower body and leg control and eventually break him down for a leg or hip lock.

Chicken Position

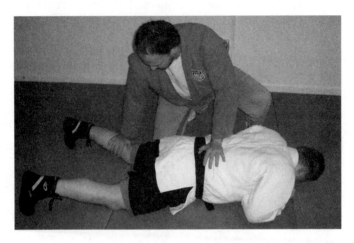

When your opponent is laying flat on his front with his arms tucked in or up around his neck, he's telling you a lot about his lack of ability in groundfighting! This is what I call the "Chicken Position." It's a weak position on the mat and not one I recommend! As you can see in this photo, the bottom man, Eric, is laying flat on his face and pretty much at the mercy of Steve, who can work a lot of offensive moves from here, not the least of which are leglocks. This position is taken by an opponent who is very defensive, is usually not skilled in groundfighting or may be tired and trying to take a rest. Sometimes in sambo matches, the bottom grappler in the chicken position may cross his ankles thinking that will somehow stop the top fighter from securing an ankle or leg lock. Crossing your ankles simply gives your opponent another ankle to lock. No matter why he gets in this position, it's a bad thing for the bottom man if the top grappler knows what to do! The bottom man in the chicken position lays flat on his face much like an ostrich who sticks his head in the sand and hopes a threat will go away. The threat doesn't go away, he simply takes advantage of the grappler who hides like this and sets him up for a submission hold! If you're the top grappler, you might want to say a silent thank you when your opponent lays flat in the chicken position. Sometimes, an opponent may roll over onto his front after you have thrown him trying to lessen the score of the throw. This is also a good time to take advantage of this chicken position. There is usually no real good reason to end up in the chicken position other than temporarily being there to see what your opponent might do.

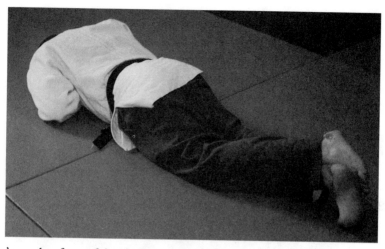

Here's another form of the chicken position that is sometimes seen in sambo. I've personally seen opponents lie flat on their fronts, hook their ankles together and hope for the best. When a grappler does this, he's banking on the notion that his two ankles hooked together are strong enough to keep his opponent from controlling his lower body with his arms and hands.

Top (Standing) Ride

This is a ride position that is similar to the wrestler's ride, but the attacker is more upright with his knees off the mat. The idea in this position is to get behind your opponent and quickly spin around to face the bottom man's feet and legs dig your feet in to break him down. There are many options for the top grappler from this position. He can work his legs in and secure a leg ride then work immediately into a rolling leglock or banana split (hip lock) or flatten the bottom man out onto his face and stomach into the chicken position, then go for another ankle or leg lock. The important thing is that the top grappler, Steve, should immediately work behind his opponent as shown so that he can control the position better.

Bottom Position on Elbows and Knees

Notice in this photo that the bottom man, Steve, is on his elbows and knees and not on his hands and knees. It's wise for the bottom grappler to be in this position and not straighten his arms. Steve is in a defensive position and knows it, so to increase his chances of getting out of this position and out of trouble, he keeps his arms bent, close to his body, hips as low as possible and stays on his toes so he can move quickly to initiate a way to get from the bottom. From this bottom position on his elbows and knees, Steve can also sit into the guard position, closing the distance between his body and Bill's and try to get close enough to lace one of Bill's legs with his legs to try to secure a leg or ankle lock.

Knee in Opponent's Crotch

Jarrod is jamming his left knee and shin into Sean's crotch and abdomen to exert as much control on the center of Sean's body as possible. Jamming your knee and shin into his crotch diverts your opponent's attention from the attack or set up you plan on doing as well! Jamming your knee in your opponent's crotch also enables you to develop a good, stable base so you can control his body more effectively. It also gets your knee in the middle of his body so you can work it in as you slide or roll into a leglock.

Rodeo Ride (Get Your Hooks In)

The rodeo ride is one of the best positions possible to set an opponent up for most any submission technique or hold-down. This is a position you should work on and work on a lot! You have almost total control of your opponent's body and something as equally important…you have his back. The rodeo ride (shown in this photo) is achieved when the top wrestler has successfully gone behind his opponent, dug his feet in his opponent's crotch and "got his back." Steve has his hooks in and has dug his feet into Bill's hips and crotch. Steve is controlling the lower body well and is careful to not hook his feet together at the ankles, as this doesn't give as much control of his opponent's body. Steve is using his hips to drive into Bill, which helps control Bill even more. Steve can rock Bill forward and this will make Bill's feet and hips pop up in the air giving Bill no control of his lower body. The rodeo ride is a good example of "leg wrestling. " Steve has flattened Bill out and broken him down from Bill's initial position on his elbows and knees. This is a strong position for the top grappler! If nothing else, it gives the top grappler some time to assess the situation and work for further control. As a continuation of the rodeo ride, in every aspect of groundfighting, you need to control your opponent's lower body (his hips and legs) before you can work any submission technique, whether they are chokes, armlocks, and leglocks. If you don't, he can shuck you off or escape easily. Don't be in too much of a hurry to apply a submission hold until you control his legs and hips. By controlling your opponent's lower body, you have good control of his entire body.

Fighting From the Guard

Many grapplers may prefer to fight from this position, and if you do, make sure that you are active and aggressive. You can set up a fair amount of ankle and knee locks from this position, so it's worth your time to work on. This is an old position from the early days of judo and it has stood the test of time. Notice that the grappler on the right in the photo, Trevor, is on his buttocks and using his feet and legs as if they were his hands and arms, pushing on Bryan's hips to control the distance while Trevor starts to go for Bryan's left ankle. The rule of thumb is that if the grappler who is in the guard wants to be aggressive, he should close the space between the two bodies and if he wants to be defensive, he should open the space and attempt to escape or get to his feet. While this is often true, sometimes the bottom grappler may close the space to keep his opponent from doing too much.

This photo shows Bill fighting from his buttocks in the guard position and controlling Steve. Bill is doing a lot of things right, but most of all he realizes he has a lot of options fighting from this position as long as he stays as round as possible and remains mobile. Bill is using his feet and legs in the same way he would his hands and arms and is also controlling the space between his body and Steve's. Remember, when you are fighting off your buttocks in the guard position to be as active as possible and as aggressive as possible so the top grappler doesn't get past your feet and legs and stick you on the mat.

Stay Round

Quite often, you will have to roll your opponent into position to leglock him. For this reason, make it a habit to "stay round." Work on your flexibility so that you can roll in most any direction with ease to control your opponent. There's more on rolling to gain momentum a bit later in this section.

Face the Back End Fast

Quickly get to business and face the business end of your partner so you can manipulate his lower extremities and break him down to apply an ankle, leg or hip lock.

Control Your Opponent's Ankle and Foot

As you break your opponent down, snatch onto an ankle or foot and go for the submission technique. The ankle is a good point to control. As shown in this photo, Steve has pulled Bill's ankle and flattened Bill out. Steve has compromised Bill's stable position by controlling his ankle and can now work for more control or go for the ankle lock or toehold.

Follow Through from a Throw or Takedown

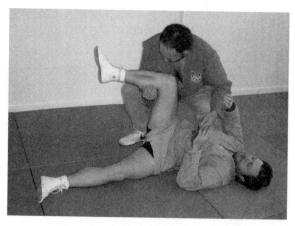

As soon as your opponent hits the mat from a throw or takedown, or even if he's slipped and fallen without you causing it, immediately finish him on the ground. A leglock is an unexpected follow-up to a throw or takedown and the element of surprise is on your side. Whether you follow through to a submission technique or a hold-down, make sure your opponent is finished off on the ground!

Control the Space

It's important to be aware of how close or how far you are from your opponent. You need "working room" to maneuver into a set-up or defensive action against your opponent. Usually, if you are the aggressor, you will want to close the distance between you and your opponent and if you are the defender, you will want to increase the space between your bodies. While this is generally true, it's not always the case and in some instances you may have to close into your opponent tightly to keep him from applying a move on you. In this photo, Trevor has his feet in Bryan's hips and is keeping Bryan at a good distance so he can maneuver to get a better position so he can attack Bryan's ankle or lace his leg.

Leg Wrestling and Leg Rides (Get Your Hooks In)

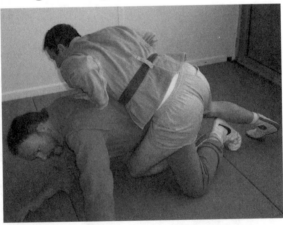

Using your legs to control and manipulate your opponent is an important skill. There are many ways to control and manipulate your opponent using your legs, feet and hips. A common skill in leg wrestling that comes from Russian Sambo is "lacing" which is shown later in this section. Shawn is using his left leg to control Steve's left leg in a near leg ride to set him up for a bent knee lock. Using your legs to control your opponent before applying the actual leg or ankle lock is also called a "Leg Ride."

Scramble Position

Often when fighting on the ground, you and your opponent will "scramble" to see who can get each other's foot or leg first. Some people call this the "Leg to Leg" position. The scramble position could start from any angle or situation, but always ends up with both grapplers facing each other as shown in this photo usually sitting on their buttocks as Rusty and Travis are. While it may look like two grapplers rolling around in an unorganized situation, both are doing their best to get their hips in close to each other for better leverage and to better reach theopponent's foot or leg. Both are doing their best to grab the opponent's foot or leg and manipulate it so he can apply a submission technique.

Lace His Legs

In much the same way you would lace up a boot or shoe to make sure it's tight, you should "lace" your opponent's leg with your legs. This phrase comes from Russian Sambo and pretty well describes what you are doing. This photo shows Jarrod controlling Sean's leg by lacing his leg using (in this case) a figure 4 or triangle lock. Lacing your opponent's legs is another measure of controlling him and setting him up for the submission. It's desirable to use both of your legs to lace one of your opponent's legs so you have the strength and control of using your two legs against only one of his, but in some cases, you may use only one of your legs to lace his leg (this is often the case in leg rides) or use each of your legs to lace and control each of your opponent's legs (as is used when taking a standing opponent to the mat if you are on your back or from the guard).

In this photo, Shawn is using his left leg to lace Steve's left leg. By using his left foot to anchor and control Steve's left leg and ankle, Shawn's near leg ride is isolating Steve's left leg and hip to set him up for the bent knee lock. This shows how lacing is another way of using good leg wrestling when setting your opponent up for a leglock.

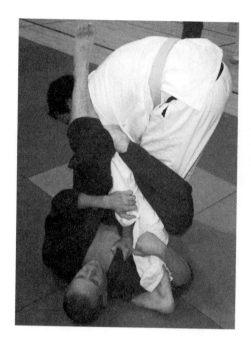

Here's another photo of Jarrod lacing Sean's leg from the guard position. Much like a cobra wraps around its prey and tightens up to finish it off, you should lace your legs around your opponent's leg and gain further control of him.

Look for the Leg or Foot (Go Fishing)

As if you have radar, focus in on the foot you want to lock! By doing this, you create opportunities and take advantage of those that may crop up unexpectedly. In the same way an angler tries to land a big catch, you "go fishing" for his foot or ankle until you land it and sink your move in on him. In this photo, Jarrod has keyed in on Chris's foot immediately after taking him to the mat and secured the toehold.

Flatten Your Opponent Out

You may not always want to roll your opponent to gain momentum or pressure. Sometimes, the best thing is to flatten him out, usually (but not always) on his front. This is a classic example of a breakdown where you take your opponent from a stable to an unstable position and take advantage of it. In this photo, Shawn has flattened Steve onto his front to control Steve's body and isolate his leg and is applying a near leg bent knee lock

In this photo, Will has turned Bret over and is flattening him out to apply a Boston Crab.

Here's a situation where you can flatten your opponent out while he is on his back and apply a leglock. Jarrod is squatting and putting his weight onto Sean to pin him to the mat to better control Sean's movement so Jarrod can better isolate Sean's leg. Here's a situation where you may not flatten your opponent onto his front side, but rather onto his back, restraining him.

Squeeze Your Legs Together

Not only do you want to squeeze your knees together, but also your upper legs as well to better trap your opponent's leg when applying an ankle or knee lock. By squeezing your legs together, this isolates his leg, making it a bit easier for you to get him to tap out. I've discussed the concept of "lacing" earlier and this is another form of it. Rather than wrapping your legs around your opponent's leg, you trap his leg with your knees and upper legs and can sometimes get the same control of his leg. This is really effective when you apply an ankle lock and roll back to apply the pressure to get the quick tap out.

Roll Back and Arch Your Hips to Apply Pressure

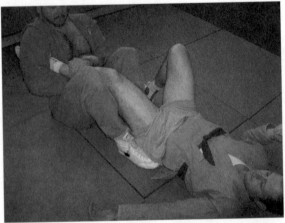

Keeping your feet under his buttocks is a good way to avoid having your opponent grab your ankle or leg to counter. If you don't give him a foot to grab, he can't use it against you. To apply more pressure, make sure you roll back and arch your hips. Use the weight of your body to apply pressure instead of just your arms.

Don't Give Up Your Ankle or Leg and the Who's Got Who Position

Sometimes, when lacing an opponent's leg, you may fall victim to having him lace your leg as well. If at all possible, try not to extend your leg too far out toward your opponent. When you and your opponent have each other's feet or ankles, this is what I call the "Who's Got Who" position. The logical (and most often used) counter to your opponent's ankle lock is to grab his ankle and apply an ankle lock on him at the same time! Often, this situation ends up in a Gator Roll and one grappler will eventually be able to tighten his hold better than his opponent and get the tap out.

One Thing Leads to Another

This is what my good friend, Jim Schneweis, calls "action-reaction-action." It's also called "chain wrestling." Basically, work one move into another to ultimately get the move you want. In this photo, Jarrod has Chris in a side hold and is working to get the near leg knee crank to finish Chris off and get the tap out.

Patience is a Virtue

Work methodically and don't rush things. Go logically and methodically from step A to step B to step C and don't skip any steps. I always like to tell my athletes; "Take your time, but do it in hurry!" What I mean is to work methodically, but don't dawdle. Be as efficient as possible in your body movement, go for the high percentage move and get the job done. In this photo, Trevor is methodically working for more control of Bryan's lower leg and ankle, all the while gaining more and more control until he eventually secures the ankle lock. Good ground-fighting isn't flashy or fancy. It's "blue collar" grappling in the truest sense!

A Good Base

Whether you are grappling on the ground or in a standing position, you must have a good, solid base from which to work. A grappler needs a solid base just like a house needs a solid foundation. If you're not stable, then you can't control your opponent. This photo shows how Steve has rolled Bill over onto his front, flattened him out and has established a strong base on his knees and left elbow to better attack Bill's left ankle.

Distract Him With Pain and the Knee Press Position

This photo shows two important things; how to distract your opponent with pain as well as how to use your knee in your opponent's chest or side in the knee press position. Sometimes, you have to distract your opponent by causing some physical discomfort to make a move work. It's not always the case, but there are some definite situations where you have to distract your opponent so that you can set him up for a leg lock. As you can see in this photo, Jarrod is jamming his knee in Chris's chest and armpit to set up the toehold. By using the knee press position, Jarrod is not only immobilizing Chris, but he is also using the pain caused to distract Chris's attention away from the foot that is being attacked. Submission grappling, judo, jujitsu, sambo, mixed martial arts and other forms of personal combat are physically hard. You have to do what is necessary to get the job done.

Everything is a Handle

Consider every part of your opponent's body and workout uniform as if it is a handle. In fact, use any and every part of your own body and attire as you would a handle! In this photo, Chris is controlling Bob's lower body and using Bob's left ankle to set him up to flatten him out. Also notice that Chris is pushing on Bob's right knee and upper leg for more control. Chris is also using his left side armpit and arm to trap Bob's body so he can better control Bob's legs. Chris is using any body part of his or his opponent's to better control the situation and set his opponent up for a leglock.

Apply Constant Pressure

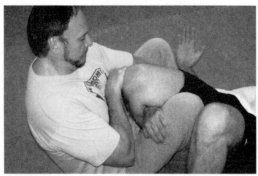

In the same way a pressure cooker creates steam to cook food, you must create your own steam by constantly applying pressure on your opponent! Work for your best position, then work for the best set up or breakdown and keep creating opportunities to get his leg. Don't let up on him; grind him and make him dislike every second he's on the mat with you. Even if he manages to get away, make him wish he had never seen you. Often you can create constant pressure by rolling him or flattening him out. There's nothing fancy or pretty about it, but it gets the job done. In this photo, Steve has applied a bent knee lock on Greg and is using his arm to jam under Greg's knee creating more pressure as he leans back.

Roll Your Opponent to Create Momentum

An effective way of creating more pressure and control is to roll your opponent to gain momentum. This is true for any ankle, knee or hip lock. Basically, you keep rolling him as you tighten your ankle, leg or hip lock. By rolling him, you gain momentum and have a good chance of making your leglock tighter and more effective as you roll. In this photo, Steve has a straight ankle lock on Bill and is rolling him to tighten the effect of the lock. I often refer to this as the "Gator Roll" but it's called other things such as the "Death Roll" or "Croc Roll" because of how an alligator or crocodile (not sure which one does it, or if both do it) takes their prey under water and rolls them before devouring them.

Split and Stretch His Legs

A good way to isolate and control the leg you are attacking is to split your opponent's legs apart and stretch him out. This can prevent him from rolling out of the attack or reaching for you and grabbing your upper body in an attempt to defend against your leglock. This also is a good angle to apply your leg or ankle lock from because his leg is at an angle and not in a straight line from his hips.

SECTION TWO
Ankle and Foot Locks & Defense

"Go for the high percentage moves. They win matches."
Bill West, U.S. National Judo Champion

From my experience, the most reliable lower body and leg submissions are the ones aimed against the ankle or foot. It seems that the farther the part of the body is away from the chest area, the easier it is to control it and the foot is about as far away from the chest as a body part can get.

When attacking the ankle or foot, the primary point to inflict pain is the ankle, either by twisting it or stretching it. An exception is the heel hook where you control and attack the heel of your opponent, but in reality, this is a variation of an ankle twist.

The three most often used foot submissions are the straight ankle lock, the toehold and the heel hook.

Straight Ankle Lock

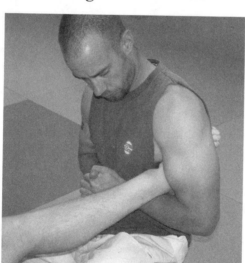

This is the fundamental ankle lock that I teach my athletes. It's got a high ratio of success and is pretty simple and straightforward. Basically, you hook under your opponent's lower leg just above the ankle joint as Kyle is doing in this photo. Notice that Kyle has the top of Ben's right foot wedged tightly in his left armpit and is cradling Ben's right ankle in his left arm. Kyle is using his left forearm to tighten up and roll the bone of his forearm against Ben's Achilles' tendon which is located immediately on the back of his lower leg. Kyle is stretching Ben's foot as he applies a lot of pressure on Ben's Achilles' tendon. The action of stretching the ankle in a straight line with the lower leg and applying a lot of pressure on the Achilles' tendon causes pain.

Heel Hook

The heel hook is a common and effective leglock. When doing a heel hook, make sure you cradle your opponent's lower leg, ankle and foot tightly between your body and arms. When applying pressure, rotate your body and let the weight of your body do the work, not only your arms. When it comes to a strength match, your opponent's leg will usually beat out both of your arms, so use your body to make this move work. It not only does a real job on your opponent's ankle, it can cause severe damage to his knee as well! Heel hooks are dangerous and many submission grappling events have made them illegal because of the severity of damage they inflict. In spite of all the negative things association with this technique, it's still an effective, hardcore submission hold and should be studied by anyone who is serious about lower body submissions.

Toehold

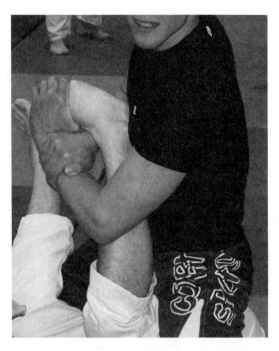

The great wrestling champion Frank Gotch made this hold famous. Basically, anytime you grab your opponent's toes or the side of his foot, it's a toehold. As shown in this photo, you grab his foot and twist the ankle, causing pain. As with the heel hook, it's important to cradle your opponent's foot between your body and arms and let the rotation of your body do the work for you. You can use the strength of your hands and arms to twist your opponent's foot, but you will get more power into the technique (and a better ratio of success) if you hug his foot, apply your hold and let the weight of your body do the work.

STRAIGHT ANKLE LOCKS

Straight ankle locks may be the group of leg submissions that has the highest ratio of success. When I say "straight" I mean any ankle lock that is stretched and in a straight line with the leg. There are two basic variations of the straight ankle lock. The first is grabbing your opponent's ankle with a figure 4 lock and the second is grabbing your opponent's ankle with a square lock. In both variations, you apply constant pressure on your opponent's Achilles' heel as you lean back and apply pressure by rolling the top of your forearm on the back of his lower leg.

The Figure 4 Lock

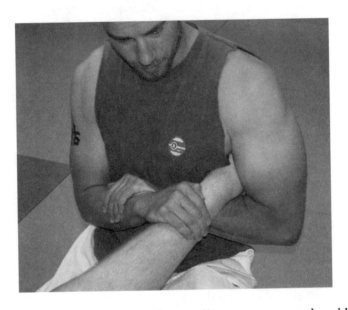

There are two primary ways of controlling an opponent's ankle when applying a straight ankle lock. This is the figure 4 method and as you can see in this photo, Kyle is using his hands in a figure 4 lock to hold Ben's right foot and leg. Kyle can add some serious pressure on Ben's ankle by pushing down with his right and on the top of Ben's lower leg and pulling up and rolling his left forearm up and against Ben's Achilles' tendon. As always in a straight ankle lock, it's important to cradle your opponent's foot in your armpit as Kyle is doing. This traps your opponent's foot in your arms, keeping his foot and leg in close and tight to your body. You can add more pressure on the ankle by arching your hips as you apply pressure to the Achilles' tendon.

Here's another figure 4 hand position. The figure 4 hand position can be applied from most any direction as Steve is doing here on Bill. This photo shows how Bill's left foot is trapped tightly into Steve's armpit so Steve can control the foot and ankle better to add more pressure to the lock.

The Square Lock

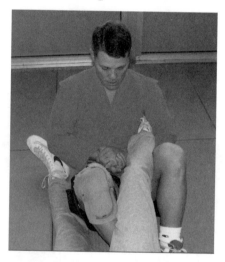

Chris is applying the square lock hand position on Steve. Some guys like the figure 4 lock and others prefer the square lock. It's really a matter of preference as both ways of locking your opponent's ankle are effective. It's always a good idea to arch your hips as you apply pressure on the ankle lock and Chris is arching his hips as he applies the pressure to Steve's Achilles' tendon by using his left forearm to squeeze and roll against the tendon.

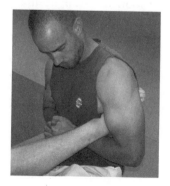

The square lock from a side view. Notice the stretch of the Achilles' tendon is made more severe with a square lock grip of the hands. Kyle is using the bone of his left forearm to squeeze and roll against the Achilles' tendon.

DEFENSE FOR LOWER BODY SUBMISSIONS

Most grapplers tend to defend their upper bodies first and this can be a costly mistake in a situation where leglocks are allowed. Honestly, the best defense is to do everything you can to be in a better position than your opponent and not give him much of a chance at taking your leg, ankle or hip.

But, when you do get caught, there are some common skills that you can try. Here are a few of them.

Leg Shoot Ankle Lock Defense and Pull on Opponent's Upper Body Defense

Rusty, on the right, is trying to get Travis's right foot in a straight ankle lock. Travis is defending by jamming his right foot hard as possible through Rusty's arms. Travis makes it a point to aim his right heel and drive it through Rusty's arms in the same way he would a kick. As he does this, Travis pulls on Rusty's jacket, pulling Rusty as close as possible to him. Travis is also doing everything possible to keep his right leg bent so Rusty can't get much leverage if he arches his hips. This is a fairly common ankle and lower foot lock.

Who Has Who Defense

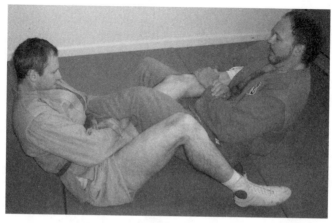

In many scramble situations, the first guy who secures the ankle or leg lock will be the winner. Make it an instinctive movement to go for your opponent's foot or ankle as soon as you realize you've been had and he has started to secure his leg or ankle lock. Honestly, in many cases, the best defense for a leg or ankle lock is to make sure your legs are bent and you know where they are in relation to your position on the mat and you will be able to avoid your opponent's attempts at slapping on a leg or ankle lock. Always attempt to keep your toes on the mat and control the movement of your feet when grappling. Don't ever relax your feet. Keep them cocked and poised and move off the balls of your feet.

Push With Your Foot Defense

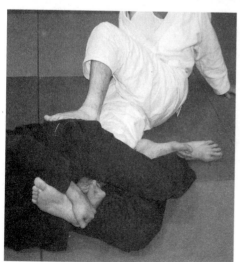

In many situations, when your opponent is going for a leglock or ankle lock, you can use your other foot and leg to push him away or manipulate him. In this photo, Sean is using his left foot to push against Jarrod to minimize the effect of the ankle lock Jarrod is applying. Notice that Sean has cocked his right foot to keep Jarrod from applying an Achilles' tendon lock.

ANKLE LOCKS

Anytime you control your opponent's ankle and apply pressure in a straight line with his leg, this is a straight ankle lock. Often, the pressure you apply on your opponent's Achilles' tendon is the cause of the pain. Ankle locks are the workhorse of lower body submissions and use often in sambo and submission grappling matches.

Straight Ankle Lock from Sambo Chest Hold

Steve has Bill held down but Bill has broken contact and is attempting to escape from the hold. As Bill pushes Steve away, Steve leans back, making sure his knees are wide for a stable base and opens the space between his body and Bill's.

Here's another view of how Bill has pushed Steve away. Notice that Steve is still holding Bill's sleeve with his left hand, but has started to uses his left elbow to slip back and hold Bill's right leg next to Steve's left side.

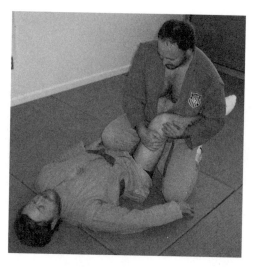

Steve snatches Bill's right leg with his left arm as shown in this photo and pulls it in tightly to his left side. As Steve does this, he rises up and gets onto his right foot, jamming his right knee hard in Bill's crotch. This knee in the crotch provides Steve with some stability and creates a distraction to Bill, taking his attention off his right leg. Notice how Steve has trapped Bill's right knee with both of his hands to his side.

Steve uses his left arm to hook under Bill's right leg and slides his left arm down to Bill's ankle as Steve leans back. Steve has now assumed a squatting position and makes sure to keep his knees pinched together around Bill's right leg. Steve makes sure to drive his left forearm directly under Bill's right Achilles' tendon.

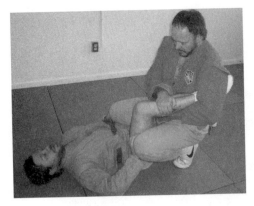

Steve has controlled Bill's lower leg and ankle with a figure 4 hold and pulls Bill's right ankle in tightly to his left side. As he does this, Steve starts to roll backward.

Steve has rolled backward and arched his hips immediately stretching Bill's right ankle making sure to cinch tightly on Bill's right Achilles' tendon causing pain in the ankle. Steve keeps his knees squeezed together to trap Bill's right leg. Notice that Steve's feet are firmly tucked under Bill's buttocks. This is to keep Bill from grabbing Steve's ankle as a counter.

Gator Roll (Standard Roll) Ankle Lock

Rolling an opponent to gain momentum and add pressure to the leg or ankle locks is a common skill that every grappler should know. Trevor has a straight ankle lock on Bryan's left ankle.

Trevor keeps rolling to his left, all the while cinching in tighter on Bryan's left ankle. You can see how Bryan's left foot is trapped under Trevor's right armpit. This photo also shows that Bryan is trying to counter Trevor's ankle lock with one of his own.

This shows a typical gator roll in action. Both grapplers are working for the advantage, but Trevor still has the upper hand with better control of Bryan's ankle. Bryan is actively going for his own ankle lock at this point.

Trevor keeps rolling and as he does, arches his hips to add more pressure to the ankle lock. Trevor has rolled Bryan over with his gator roll and the momentum of the roll has cinched the ankle lock in really tight, forcing the tap out.

Gator Roll if Opponent Defends Ankle Lock

If you've attempted a straight ankle lock and your opponent defends by jamming his foot forward and pulls on your jacket (or you) to ease the pressure, quickly start to roll to get the ankle lock.

In this photo, Travis has jammed his right foot through Rusty's arms and has pulled on his jacket to ease the pressure of Rusty's ankle lock.

Rusty rolls to his left side which forces Travis's right foot up and deeper into Rusty's left arm. This rolling action also cranks Travis's right knee unnaturally.

Rusty continues to roll and the momentum of his rolling helps in securing Travis's right foot and leg and causes pressure on Travis's ankle and knee.

Gator Roll (North-South Variation)

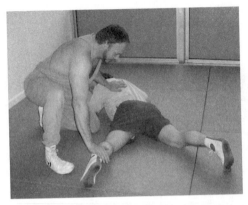

Here's a pretty basic move, but one that will work for you when you need it. Bill is on his front in the chicken position and Steve is at his side. Steve quickly turns to face Bill's feet.

Steve is now in the north-south position and using his right knee to stabilize himself. Steve is starting to reach for Bill's left ankle.

Steve uses his right arm to hook over Bill's left foot and hug it tightly into his armpit as shown. Steve's left foot is posted on the mat wide and away from Bill's body so Bill can't reach for it very easily.

As Steve rolls to his left, he scoops Bill's left foot in even tighter and grabs his hands in a square lock. Steve uses his right forearm to place pressure on Bill's left Achilles' tendon. Notice how Steve's left knee has bent and he has swung it under himself to add momentum to his roll.

Steve is in the middle of the gator roll and arching his hips really hard to add pressure to the ankle lock. As Steve rolls, the momentum of the rolling action adds pressure to the ankle lock and gets the tap out.

North-South Ankle Lock

Bill is on all fours in a fairly stable position. Steve is breaking Bill down from this stable position by using his left hand to hook under Bill's waist (Steve is using his left hand to grab Bill's far hip) and using his right hand to hook Bill's left ankle and pull it out.

Steve breaks Bill down to his front by pulling hard with his right hand on Bill's left ankle and driving into Bill with his left shoulder.

Steve keeps hold of Bill's left ankle with his right hand and quickly turns to face Bill's feet.

Steve posts on his right knee and left hand for stability as he hooks his right arm over Bill's left ankle and tucks it in his right armpit as shown.

Steve steps over Bill's body with his left knee and rests it on the mat. As he does this, Steve is in a direct north-south position with Bill. Steve uses a figure 4 arm position on Bill's left ankle. Notice that Bill's left leg is still bent. This makes Bill's leg a weaker target for Steve.

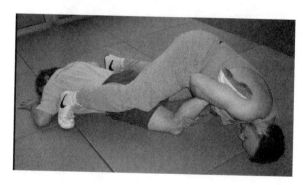

Steve can now either stretch out to apply pressure as shown here or start his gator roll.

Cuban Leg Grab Takedown to Ankle Lock

Shawn attacks Steve with a Cuban Leg Grab to take him to the mat. The Cuban Leg Grab is a single leg throw where Shawn scoops high on Steve's leg and drives him directly backward. It's more than a takedown and is really a hard throw. Shawn is using his left arm to hook Steve's left leg.

As Shawn takes Steve to the mat, he quickly moves to his right so he can get to Steve's left side. Notice that Shawn's left knee is starting to bend and he is driving it close to Steve's left inner thigh for more control of Steve's left leg. Shawn keeps good control of Steve's left leg with his left arm holding just above Steve's left knee.

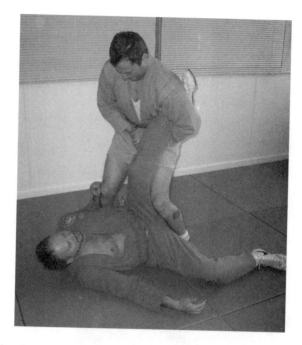

Shawn grabs his hands together in a square lock securing Steve's left lower leg and ankle in Shawn's left armpit. As Shawn does this, he pinches his knees together to trap Steve's left leg. Shawn stands up straighter and arches his hips to get more pressure to the straight ankle lock. Sometimes, this is enough to get the tap out, but not always. Usually, Shawn will have to sit on his buttocks and roll onto his back to make the move work better.

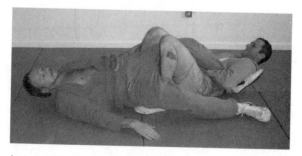

Shawn sits back onto his buttocks and rolls onto his back as he squeezes his knees tightly around Steve's left leg. As Shawn rolls back, he arches his hips and places a lot of pressure on Steve's left Achilles' tendon with his left forearm. This action of rolling back places a lot of pressure on Steve's ankle and leg.

Korean Ankle Pick to Ankle Lock

This ankle pick was named the Korean Ankle Pick because it was popular among many Korean judo athletes in the 1960s and 1970s.

John has used his right foot to wrap around Chance's right foot as shown. John is bending his right knee and driving it on the inside of Chance's right shin and lower leg. John's knee and foot trap Chance's right foot. As John does this, he reaches down with his left hand to scoop Chance's right ankle. Notice John's right arm is hooked under Chance's left arm and shoulder.

John uses his left hand to grab Chance's right ankle and pull it to John's left hip. As John does this, he drives Chance down with his right hand, throwing Chance to the mat. This is more than a takedown and is a hard throw really.

John uses his left hand to swing Chance's right foot across John's body as shown. As he does this, John is getting ready to hook under Chance's right leg with his right arm.

John hooks over Chance's right leg with his right arm and secures Chance's right foot in John's right armpit. As John does this, he quickly moves his left leg by Chance's right hip and as John starts to sit back onto his buttocks, he jams his left foot in Chance's right hip.

John arches his hips really hard as he rolls backward using a square lock to grab his hands together. John has squeezed both his knees together to trap Chance's right leg.

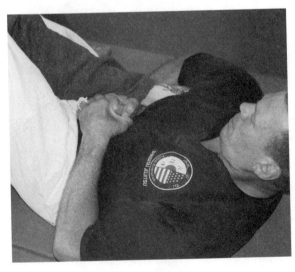

Here's a closer view of how John has grabbed his hands together in a square lock and is using his right forearm to wrench Chance's right Achilles' tendon.

Single Leg Takedown to Ankle Lock (Ankle to Ankle)

I call this "Ankle to Ankle" because you're attacking your opponent with an ankle pick and never letting go of it, eventually turning it into a straight ankle lock.

Chris has shot in for a single leg takedown and is using his right hand to grab the back of Brian's left foot at the ankle.

Chris takes Brian down with the ankle pick. Notice that Chris has pulled Brian's left ankle with his right hand to Chris' right hip. At this point, Chris makes sure to place Brian's left foot securely on his right hip so he can start to work on the ankle lock.

Chris quickly does a figure 4 hold (but can just as easily do a square lock with his hand) to secure Brian's left ankle.

Chris uses his left knee to jam in between Brian's legs in Brian's crotch as shown. As he does this, Chris starts to bend both legs and pinch his knees together to trap Brian's left leg.

Chris sits on his buttocks and rolls onto his back making sure to pinch his knees together to keep Brian's left leg trapped. As he rolls back, Chris arches his hips and applies the straight ankle lock on Brian's left ankle.

Double Leg Takedown to Ankle Lock

Jarrod shoots in deep for a double leg takedown on Sean.

As Jarrod takes Sean to the mat, he makes sure to keeps both of his arms tight around Sean's thighs. This keeps Sean from moving away or shrimping to try to pull Jarrod into his guard.

Jarrod quickly moves up and jams his left knee into Sean's crotch. As he does this, Jarrod used both of his arms to grab Sean's belt.

Jarrod keeps his left knee jammed in Sean's crotch as he uses his right arm to slide down Sean's left leg and grab the ankle. Jarrod maintains good control of Sean by keeping a firm grip with his left hand on Sean's belt. Jarrod uses his left arm to hook over Sean's left ankle as shown.

Jarrod quickly pinches his knees together to trap Sean's left leg and Jarrod uses a figure 4 hand hold to secure Sean's left ankle for a straight ankle lock. Jarrod can either roll directly back onto his buttocks then onto his back or add more pressure by doing this, then rolling to his right hip as shown.

Scissors Ankle Lock (Figure 4)

Here's why everybody tells you to never cross your ankles when you're behind your opponent in a seated rodeo ride! Eric is behind Bret in a rodeo ride and going for a choke. He's made the mistake of crossing his ankles to attempt to squeeze Bret to control him better.

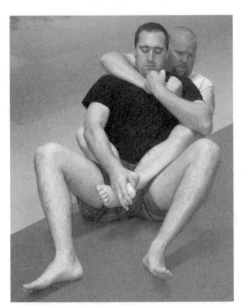

As Bret fights off Eric's choke with his left hand, he uses his right hand to push down on Eric's right ankle. Bret may also pull Eric's right ankle out a bit to better set it up for the move to come.

Bret quickly uses his left leg to hook over Eric's right ankle as shown in this photo. Bret now can use both hands to fight off Eric's choke. Bret is using his left lower leg to push down on Eric's right ankle and this starts the ankle lock.

Bret adds more pressure to the ankle lock by doing a triangle (also called a figure 4) leg position. Bret has jammed the top of his left foot under his right knee. As he does this, Bret uses his left lower leg to really put a lot of pressure on Eric's ankle. Bret can add more pressure by driving his right foot down.

Here is a top view of the figure 4 ankle lock. You can see how Eric's right foot is trapped and being bent downward causing pain in the ankle joint.

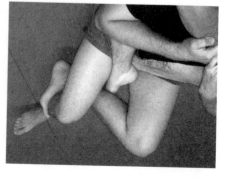

Scissors Ankle Lock (Push Foot)

Here's a nasty little move that really hurts. Kyle has Ben in a rodeo ride and has crossed his ankles. Kyle's left ankle is on top. Ben uses his hands and arms to pull Kyle's knees into him for better control.

Ben uses his left leg to hook over the top of Kyle's left ankle. Ben uses his right hand to pull his left foot up and over Kyle's left ankle. Ben uses his left hand and arm to scoop Kyle's left leg in tighter to his body for more control.

Ben uses his right foot to push down on his left foot just above his ankle. By doing this, Ben exerts a great deal of pressure on Kyle's left foot as shown and causes pain in the ankle.

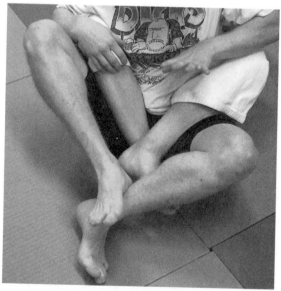

Here's a closer view of how Ben is using his right foot to push down on his left ankle and lower leg to trap Kyle's foot. You can see how this wrenches Kyle's left foot to the left and produces pain in the joint.

Ankle Lock from the Guard

This is a common ankle lock from the guard position. Trevor is fighting off his back and using his feet to push against Bryan's hips keeping him at a safe distance.

Trevor quickly rolls to his right side and uses his right arm to hook around Bryan's left ankle. Trevor is using his left hand to secure Bryan's ankle and help pull himself over to his right side. Trevor makes it a point to keep his feet in Bryan's hips.

Here's another view of how Trevor has rolled onto his right side and secured the hook around Bryan's left ankle. Trevor's feet are firmly jammed in each of Bryan's hips.

Trevor pushes Bryan backward using his feet in Bryan's hips and using his right arm to scoop Bryan's left ankle in tighter into his armpit. Trevor is using a square lock to secure the ankle and is using his right forearm to apply pressure to Bryan's left Achilles' tendon.

Spinning Ankle Lock from the Guard

Trevor has Bryan in his guard with his feet jammed in each of Bryan's hips. Also, Bryan could have stood up to try to get past Trevor's guard.

Trevor quickly curls his body to his right in a shrimping movement and makes sure to use his right hand to hook under Bryan's left lower leg and ankle. Trevor pulls his head as close to Bryan's left leg as possible so Trevor will be sideways and not straight on to Bryan. Trevor has used his left hand to grab Bryan's right arm and pull it to his chest. Trevor's right leg is jammed across the left side of Bryan's body at his ribcage.

Trevor uses his right hand and arm to hook Bryan's left lower leg and he pulls Bryan's left arm to his body using his left hand as Trevor pushes with his right leg across Bryan's body. This forces Bryan to the mat as shown.

As Bryan rolls to the mat (to his left) Trevor quickly hooks under Bryan's left lower leg using his right arm as shown. Notice that Trevor is lying on his left side with Bryan's body trapped between his legs.

Trevor uses his right forearm to hook under Bryan's left Achilles' tendon and ankle. Trevor grabs his hands together and while still lying on his left side, arches his hips to add pressure to the ankle lock.

Gator Roll Ankle Lock from Pinning Opponent on Mat

Jarrod is jamming Sean into the mat using the weight of his body and driving into him arching with his hips. Jarrod is holding onto Sean's jacket with both of his hands and driving Sean into the mat. This pins Sean to the mat so Jarrod can apply an ankle lock.

Jarrod uses his left hand to hook under Sean's left Achilles' tendon and ankle, resting his left forearm under Sean's Achilles' tendon.

Jarrod quickly uses the figure 4 grip to control Sean's lower right leg as he continues to bear his weight down on Sean pinning him to the mat. Jarrod could arch his hips forward as he cradles Sean's right ankle in his armpit and finish the ankle lock here. But if Sean hasn't tapped out, Jarrod can add momentum to the lock by starting a gator roll.

Jarrod immediately starts his gator roll to this left side to gain momentum on the ankle lock. Jarrod will roll to his left and as he does, cinch the ankle lock in tighter.

Far Ankle Breakdown to Figure 4 Ankle Lock

Here's a good move that really can take your opponent by surprise. John has used both of his hands to grab Eric's far (left) lower leg. John's left hand is hooking Eric's left ankle and John's right hand is trapping Eric's left lower leg. John is driving his right shoulder into Eric's left side and hip.

Drives hard with his right shoulder into Eric's left side as he scoops Eric's left lower leg up and into his body with his left hand. Notice how John is driving off his left foot to get extra power.

John has broken Eric down on Eric's left side. John immediately uses his left arm to hook under Eric's left foot as shown. Look at how Eric's left leg is bent. John is grabbing Eric's jacket with his left hand to trap Eric's foot. John continues to drive Eric over and onto his back.

John has broken Eric down with Eric on his back. John maintains control of Eric's jacket with his left hand trapping Eric's left foot as shown. Look at how the top of Eric's foot is resting inside the crook of John's left elbow.

Here's a closer view of how John has trapped Eric's left foot and is cranking it upward and into Eric's buttocks. This stretches Eric's ankle and causes pain.

John adds more pressure to the hold by using his right forearm to jam under Eric's neck (by holding onto Eric's collar). John is driving his right elbow upward and forcing Eric's head to turn to Eric's right. This cranks the neck and adds pressure to the entire move getting the tap out.

HEEL HOOKS

Heel hooks are extremely painful and potentially dangerous. Not only can you do serious damage to your opponent's ankle, you can do even more damage to his knee. The torque applied by hooking the heel causes considerable damage to the ligaments and tendons of the knee. For this reason, heel hooks aren't allowed in sambo competition or in some mixed martial arts events. I don't allow the guys in my club to use them when going live for safety reasons. However, heel hooks are highly effective and get the job done if you want to make your opponent tap out!

Switching From One Lock to Another

A good point to remember is that you can slap on a heel hook instead of a straight ankle lock or a toehold. Any of these ankle and foot locks are interchangeable. Another thing to consider is that you can quickly switch to a heel hook if your straight ankle lock doesn't work. Don't hesitate to switch to another foot lock if the initial attack doesn't work.

Heel Hook Position in the Arms

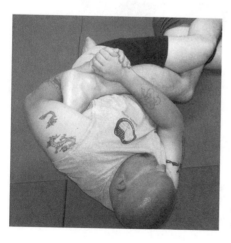

For a heel to hook to be effective, you must cradle your opponent's foot tightly in your side as shown in this photo. Eric is using his hands (locked together in what's called the "square" lock) to pull Bret's foot and lower leg tightly to his left side. Eric applies pressure to Bret's foot, ankle and leg by turning to his right as he hugs Bret's foot. Eric is allowing the turn and weight of his body to do the work which makes the lock tighter and more effective.

Leg Lace to Heel Hook

From the scramble position, Jarrod has laced Sean's right leg with a triangle. Once he has Sean's right leg isolated with the lace, Jarrod quickly uses his left arm to start to scoop Sean's right heel into the inside of his left elbow.

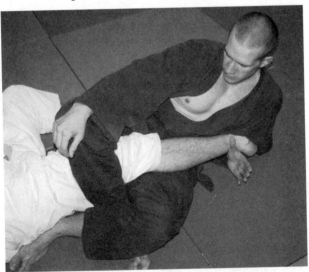

Jarrod maintains control of Sean's right leg with his lacing action (using a triangle hold) as he slides his right forearm under Sean's right heel to set up the heel hook. Sean's right foot is wedged in the inside of Jarrod's right arm and Jarrod is hugging Sean's foot tightly to his body.

Jarrod applies the heel hook, pulling Sean's right leg in tight to his body as Jarrod rolls to his back. Notice that Jarrod's left wrist is immediately under Sean's right Achilles' tendon as Jarrod applies the heel hook. Jarrod continues to keep the triangle hold on Sean's right leg to isolate it.

Notice that Jarrod's right leg is hooked over Sean's right upper leg to form the triangle that laces Sean's leg tightly. Jarrod is hugging Sean's right foot in tight to his body and arching and turning to his right, allowing the weight and turn of his body to do the work.

Double Leg Roll to Heel Hook

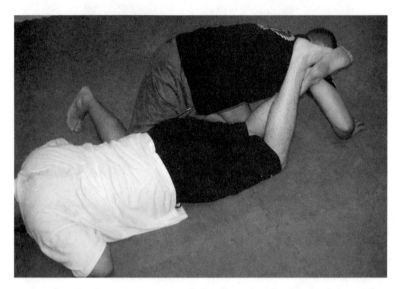

Greg is in the chicken position with his legs hooked together as shown. Bret has turned to Greg's feet and is hooking his right arm under both of Greg's feet.

Bret hooks under Greg's ankles with his right arm as shown and scoops them both in tightly to his body.

Bret has scooped both of Greg's ankles in tight to his body and trapped them with his right arm. As he does this, Bret rolls to this left side and rests on his left hip. Bret pulls Greg's legs really tight to the right side of Bret's body for maximum control of both of Greg's legs.

Bret rolls over his left side and onto his buttocks as shown as he scoops Greg's legs and feet up under his right armpit and into the right side of his torso. Notice that by rolling, Bret has Greg's legs and body between his legs. Bret makes sure to tuck both of his feet under Greg's buttocks to keep Greg from countering by grabbing Bret's ankles.

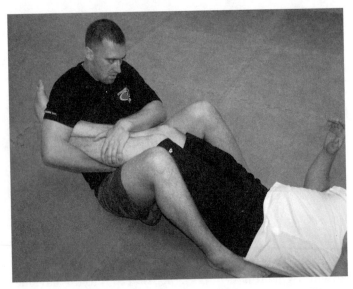

Bret sits up and pulls Greg's feet in tight to his body as shown. Bret squeezes his knees together to further trap Greg's legs, pinching them together.

Bret quickly applies a heel hook on Greg's top foot by sliding his right forearm under Greg's top (right) heel. Bret applies a square lock and hugs Greg's right foot tightly into his left side. Bret will get the tap out by twisting his upper body to his left.

Standing Heel Hook

Bret is standing up as Bill is trying to either keep him away with his feet or pull back down into his guard. As Bret stands, he uses his right hand to grab Bill's left ankle.

Bret uses his right hand to pull Bill's left foot up into Bret's right armpit. As he does this, Bret uses his right hand to hook under Bill's left heel. Bret grabs his hands together to form a square lock to secure the heel hook. Bret twists to his left as he cradles Bill's left foot in his right side forcing the tap out. Notice how Bret has used his right upper thigh and hip to help cradle Bill's left foot and secure it more tightly.

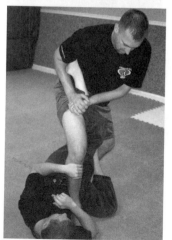

To cause more pain, Bret can step over Bill's left leg as shown causing both a heel hook and a knee crank on Bill's left leg.

Leg Lace from the Guard to Heel Hook & Knee Crank

This is a good way to get your opponent to the mat if he's standing above you. It's also a nasty "double trouble" move where you can get a heel hook and a bent knee crank. John is on his back in the guard position making sure both of his feet are wedged in Steve's hips. John uses his left hand to grab Steve's right heel and uses his right hand to grab Steve's right wrist and pull it to John's right side.

John shoots his left leg through Steve's legs, pulling himself through using his left hand on Steve's ankle. John makes sure to keep Steve's right arm pinned to his chest as he does this. Notice that Steve's right foot is next to John's left hip.

John starts to lace his left leg around Steve's right leg as shown in the photo. John's left foot is starting to lace over Steve's right hip. As he does this, John uses his right foot to hook into Steve's left knee just above the knee joint.

Here is another view of how John is starting to lace his left leg around Steve's right leg. Notice John's right foot wedged immediately under Steve' left knee.

John takes Steve down to his back and using his right hand, starts to slide down Steve's right leg to grab his heel.

Sometimes your opponent will land more on his side as Frederic has done in this photo. When this happens, it puts Frederic's right foot in the perfect position to get heel hooked as well as get a sideward crank on his right knee. John's right arm can immediately hook under Frederic's right heel. John uses his right leg to press down against Frederic's right knee (that is bent sideways) to apply pressure on both Frederic's right heel and right knee. Having your opponent land on his side doesn't always happen, but be ready when it does as you can slap on the heel hook and knee crank immediately!

John laces his left leg over Steve's knee (just above the knee joint) and uses his left forearm to trap Steve's right heel as shown. John is using his left hand to grab Steve's right lower leg. This sets up the heel hook and isolates Steve's right leg to crank the knee.

John applies the heel hook on Steve's right foot by using his right hand to cup over Steve's right heel and pulls it to John's right.

The Saylor Heel Hook

Here's a photo of the unique way John Saylor has trapped Frederic's heel. Notice that John is grabbing his pants at his left hip to anchor the heel hook in his left forearm. If it's a no gi situation and John is in a singlet or shorts, he can place his left hand (palm down) on his left thigh instead of grabbing his pants. John was the first person that I've seen to do this heel hook application back in the early 1990s. This variation really cranks the heel and adds a tremendous amount of pressure.

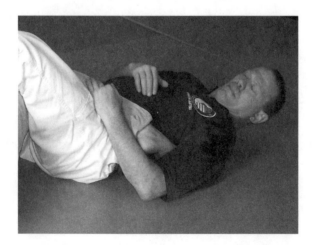

Here's another variation of how John Saylor does his heel hook.

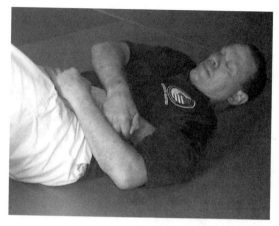

John cups his right hand over Steve's right heel and pulls it in very tightly to his chest making sure the top of Steve's right foot is placed firmly in John's left ribcage or side. As John does this, he start to turn his body to his right, wrenching Steve's right foot as he does.

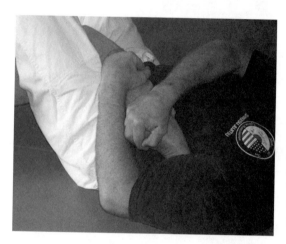

Here is a closer view of how John cups his right hand on Steve's right heel and firmly holds it in his left side. You can see that John can exert a lot of pressure on Steve's foot as John turns and rolls to his right side. John won't have to roll very much as this exerts a lot of pressure on Steve's ankle and knee.

As John rolls to his right, he not only cranks Steve's ankle but Steve's right knee as well. Believe me, this hurts!

Rolling Heel Hook

Eric is between Bret's legs in the guard position. Eric starts to pull his body backwards to give himself space to work the leglock.

Eric rises up on his left foot as shown, cradling Bret's right leg on Eric's left knee. Eric quickly grabs the outside of Bret's right foot (by Bret's toes) and as he does this, Eric uses his right hand to reach over to grab Bret's right heel.

Eric grabs his hands together to form the square lock and applies the heel hook on Bret's right foot. As he does this, Eric jams his left leg over Bret's right leg at Bret's right thigh as shown.

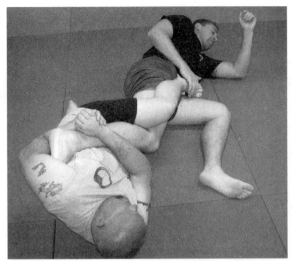

Eric rolls to his right side, keeping the heel hook in effect as he does. Eric makes sure to hug Bret's right foot tightly to his left side as he rolls to his right side and hip. This applies a lot of pressure to Bret's heel and knee and causes even more pressure with the knee crank.

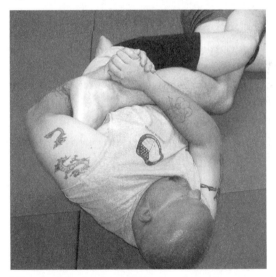

Eric has trapped Bret's right heel with his hands and arms and is applying added pressure by rolling to his (Eric's) right and clamping in tighter with his hands on Bret's ankle. As he does this, Eric is using his left elbow to lift Bret's heel and turn it to Eric's right. Also notice how Eric has Bret's ankle and foot tucked firmly in his left ribcage trapping it.

Heel Hook from a Scramble or Who's Got Who

Often, when you and your opponent are in a scramble situation, both of you are actively working to get the other guys' ankle, heel or leg and the first one who establishes a strong hold gets the tap out. When you are ever in a scramble situation, it is vital that you aggressively "fish" for your opponent's foot to gain control and secure a joint lock.

TOE HOLDS

A toehold is what happens anytime you grab onto the side, top or bottom of your opponent's foot and twist it. It's really a pretty straightforward and simple concept and it works really well. From what I've heard as well as from what I've read in various places, the first to popularize this particular way of twisting an ankle was the great professional wrestling champion Frank Gotch. Gotch wrestled in the golden age of legitimate professional wrestling and was a master of this technique.

How A Toe Hold Works

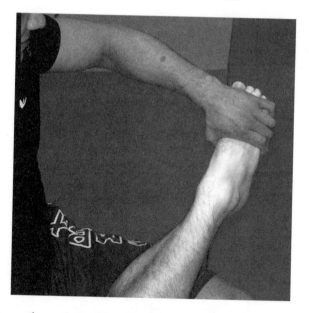

A toehold is easily explained but has many variations. Basically, anytime you grab your opponent's lower foot and twist it, it's a toehold. In this photo, Jarrod has grabbed his opponent's foot and is showing how a toehold starts.

Jarrod has used his right hand to grab Chris's right foot. Jarrod uses his right hand to hook under Chris's right ankle and will grab his right hand onto his left wrist.

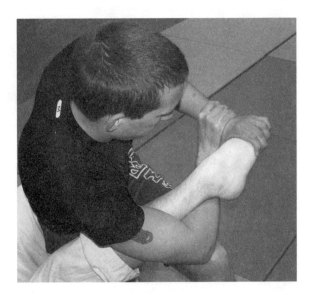

Jarrod has used his right hand to grab his left wrist to form a figure 4. Jarrod then uses his right elbow to lift up on Chris' ankle as he uses his left hand to push down on Chris's foot. This causes a twisting movement and hurts!

Toehold from a Scramble Position

Often, when grappling on the mat, both athletes will "scramble." This is when each of them are sitting on their buttocks and grabbing for their opponent's ankles or feet in an effort to secure an ankle lock, heel hook or toehold. In this situation, Chris has managed to secure an ankle lock on Jarrod and Jarrod will use a toehold to counter. Chris has his feet scissored around Jarrod's right leg.

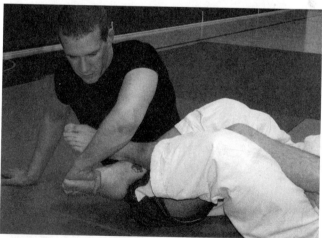

Jarrod uses his left hand to reach over and grab Chris's right (bottom) foot. Notice how Jarrod is grabbing Chris's toes and lower foot. As he does this, Jarrod makes it a point to use his right forearm to pull Chris's left (top) foot in close to his body to trap it.

Jarrod has used his right hand to reach up and under Chris's right ankle and has grabbed his left wrist forming a figure 4. Jarrod's left hand is pushing down on the top of Chris's right foot and toes. Doing this traps Chris's right foot and twists it. As he does this, Jarrod pulls both of Chris's feet in closer to him and pulls his left elbow back to his left. Doing this really adds pressure to the toehold.

Here's another view of how Jarrod is using his left hand to push down on the top of Chris's right foot and how Chris's right ankle is being twisted.

Toehold from an Ankle Pick

Jarrod and Chris are locked up and working for a takedown.

Jarrod shoots in with an ankle pick using his left hand to scoop Chris's right ankle.

Jarrod makes sure to pull Chris's right ankle to his left hip with his left hand. He does this so he can use this position to work on Chris's right foot.

Jarrod steps into Chris with his left foot as he plants Chris's right foot on his left hip for control.

Jarrod quickly reaches over and under Chris's right ankle with his right hand, sliding it toward Chris's right lower foot (at the toes) and grabbing the outside of Chris's right foot. Then Jarrod uses his right hand to grab his left wrist forming a figure 4 hand hold. Notice how Jarrod has stepped forward with his right foot with his right toes pointing outward.

Jarrod uses his right leg to step over Chris's right leg, trapping that leg to isolate it. Jarrod then uses his left hand to push down on Chris's right foot. Jarrod also pulls his right elbow toward his own body, trapping Chris's right lower leg.

Often, Jarrod will have to roll to his left hip, keeping control of Chris's right foot as he does, to secure a stronger toehold.

Toehold Against the Guard

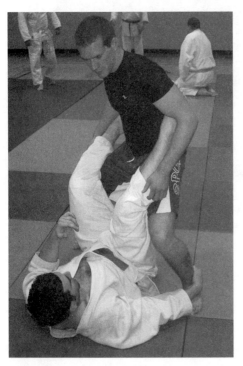

Sometimes, when your opponent has you between his legs in his guard, you can stand up to try to create distance. Other times, you might have thrown your opponent and he rolls around and placing his feet in your hips as shown Chris is on his back with Jarrod standing above him. Jarrod makes it a point to bend his knees and move in close to Chris. Jarrod uses both of his hands to grab Chris's legs and pull them onto his upper thighs.

Jarrod quickly squats directly down on the back of Chris's legs, driving with his hips. At this point, Jarrod uses his left hand to grab the outside of Chris's right foot at the toes and pull Chris's foot in close to his chest. Jarrod is using his left forearm to trap Chris's left ankle to his chest for better control.

Jarrod uses his left hand to tightly secure Chris's right foot and to pull Chris's right foot around as close to his chest as possible. As he does this, Jarrod uses his right hand to grab his left wrist and for a figure 4. Jarrod draws his right wrist and forearm close to his body to crank Chris's ankle more tightly. Notice how Jarrod is driving down with his hips and the weight of his body onto the back of Chris's thighs and buttocks to control him.

Jarrod can exert more control and get more leverage in his toehold if he jams his left knee in Chris's right side at the ribs and chest area as shown in this photo. While he's doing this, Jarrod cranks hard on the toehold.

Toehold Against the Elevator from the Guard

If Chris is attempting to use the elevator rollover from the guard position, Jarrod can counter with a toehold. Chris is using his right leg and foot to hook under Jarrod's left leg as shown.

Jarrod pulls back and squats low on his right knee to create space. Jarrod also makes sure to draw his left foot in closer to his left hip to trap Chris's right foot.

Jarrod uses his left hand to grab the top of Chris's left foot at his toes as Jarrod turns his body to his left.

Using his right hand, Jarrod reaches on the outside of Chris's right leg and knee and then under Chris's right lower leg to grab his own wrist. This creates a figure 4 with his hands. Jarrod pushes down on Chris's right foot using his left hand. Jarrod's right wrist is the lever that Jarrod is using to create the pain in the ankle.

Toehold from the Side Hold

Jarrod is on top of Chris in a side hold and Chris has scissored Jarrod's left leg as shown.

Jarrod shifts his body to his left and rests on his right hip and upper leg. Jarrod also posts on the mat with his right elbow and left hand for stability. As he does this, Jarrod places his left foot on the mat to create space and gain a more stable position.

Using his left hand, Jarrod reaches for and grabs the top of Chris' left foot, pulling it in close.

Jarrod now turns to his left and uses his right hand to also grab Chris's left foot as shown in this photo. Jarrod pulls hard on Chris's foot and as you can see, Chris's right leg is trapped and is being used as the fulcrum creating the joint lock.

Rolling Toehold

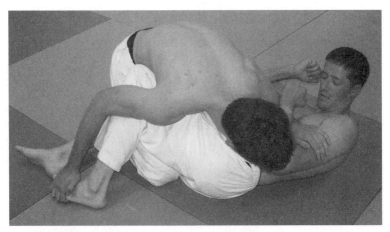

This is an effective toehold that Gene LeBell has featured in his book ENCYCLOPEDIA OF FINISHING HOLDS. It's a good way to catch an opponent who has you tied up by scissoring your legs or when you are in the half-guard position. In this photo, Travis had scissored Vince's right leg and Vince has turned to his right and used his right hand to grab the top of Travis's left foot. Vince has used his left hand to press down on Travis's left upper arm to trap it. Vince's head os positioned over Travis's left hip.

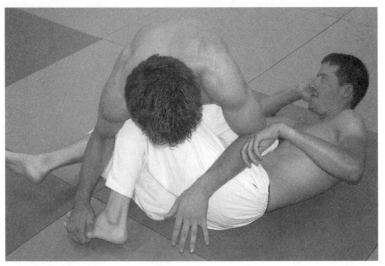

Vince uses his left hand and arm to push Travis's left hip in and as he does this, Vince starts to lift his left knee and bring it across Travis's right hip, then over both hips.

Vince jams his left knee across Travis's body as shown in this photo and will point his left knee toward Travis's feet. As he does this, Vince uses his left hand to grab his right wrist that is still holding Travis's foot at his toes. Vince's body is rolling to his left.

Vince rolls to his left across his left shoulder, arm and knee as he cinches in the figure 4 hold he has on Travis's left foot. The momentum of Vince's body rolling to his left is adding to the pressure of the toehold he has on Travis's left foot. Notice that Vince has his right leg hooked under Travis's right upper leg. Vince's left knee is jammed tightly on the side of Travis's left hip and Vince's left foot is wedged in Travis's left hip.

Vince has completed his roll and has Travis in the toehold. The rolling of Vince's body, along with the figure 4 toehold produces the desired result: a tap out.

Here's another view of the finished technique, showing how Vince has wedged his left foot in Travis's left hip which helps control Travis's left leg and hip isolating it for Vince to control to get a stronger toehold. Vince has Travis's left leg hugged tightly to his body form maximum control.

Toehold Counter to Spinning Cross-body Armlock

A toehold is a good counter to a spinning cross-body armlock. Sean has Jarrod in his guard and has used his right hand to hook under Jarrod's left knee as he attempts to shrimp in close and start a spinning cross-body armlock. Jarrod senses the danger in Sean hooking under his left knee and quickly uses his left hand to reach under Sean's right leg and grab Sean's right foot at the top outside as shown. Jarrod then uses his right hand to grab his own left hand (holding Sean's upper foot at the toes) and add pressure to the hold by pulling down.

Toehold from a Wrestler's Ride

Jarrod is riding Chris and has quickly turned to the "business end" and is using his left hand to scoop Chris's right ankle. Jarrod is in a stable position, having posted with his left leg as shown.

Jarrod now turns completely to face the back end of Chris and has continued to scoop up on Chris's right ankle with his left hand. At this point, Jarrod grabs the bottom of Chris's right foot and starts to pull it in and around to Jarrod's right toward Chris's right hip.

Jarrod quickly turns his left hand over and is pulling up on Chris's right foot as shown. Jarrod continues to use his right hand to pull up on Chris's right foot.

Here's another view of this toehold. You can see how Jarrod is using his right hand to pull Chris's right foot up and toward Chris's buttocks. Jarrod is using his left hand to pull on Chris's foot as well creating a painful toehold.

Toehold and Knee Crank from a Side Hold

This is a pretty simple and straightforward move, but one that comes in handy once in a while. Jarrod is holding Chris in a side hold and Chris is bending his near (right) leg to keep Jarrod from going over the top to mount him.

Jarrod takes advantage of this situation by using his right hand to reach for Chris's right ankle.

Jarrod hooks his right hand on top of Chris's right foot and pulls it toward him. As he does this, Jarrod jams his right elbow on the inside of Chris's right knee and jams his right shoulder on the inside of Chris's right thigh.

Jarrod has now used his right hand to reach over Chris's body and grab the top of Chris's right foot as shown. Jarrod now pulls Chris's foot toward him with a lot of force.

Here's another view of how Jarrod is pulling on Chris's right foot with both of his hands and has created both a toehold and knee crank to get the tap out.

Toehold from a Straight Knee Lock

Jarrod has rolled Chris into a cross-body leglock and is making a real effort to get the lock to take effect.

Chris has managed to get onto a more stable position on his right hip and pulled away, lessening the effect of the leglock. As Chris does this, Jarrod quickly uses his right hand to grab Chris's right ankle really close to the heel of the foot. Jarrod also uses his left hand to grab the top of Chris's foot as shown in this photo.

Jarrod forms a figure 4 with his hand to secure Chris's foot and ankle in a toehold. Jarrod rests his right elbow on the mat for stability as he uses his right hand to grab his left wrist. Jarrod's left hand is holding the top of Chris's foot and pushing it downward creating pain in the joint.

Near Leg Ride from the Guard to a Toehold

John has Steve in his guard and is up on his buttocks as he uses his right hand to reach over Steve's right shoulder to grab his belt. John also has used his left hand to hold Steve's right elbow and pull it close to John's body. John's right leg is between Steve's legs and his left leg is positioned as shown.

John rolls hard to his right side as he scoots his body out from beneath Steve's. As he does this, John starts to uses his right leg to hook on the inside of Steve's right inner thigh and upper leg.

John now comes on the outside of Steve's body and is seated on his buttocks as shown. Notice that John has laced his right leg on the inside of Steve's right leg and is using his right foot to draw Steve's right leg in as tight as possible. John is pulling on Steve's belt with his right hand and driving Steve forward.

John now laces his right leg hard inside Steve's right leg in a near leg ride. As he does this, John uses his right elbow to jam in Steve's right rear end and uses his right hand to grab Steve's right foot as shown.

John now does a near leg bent knee lock by pulling with both hands on Steve's right foot. John uses his left foot to push on his own right ankle or heel to help create a powerful bent knee lock on Steve's right leg. Notice that John has rocked back onto his back and forced Steve to flatten out onto his front.

John can use a toehold from this bent knee lock position by shifting his right hand and forearm onto the inside of his opponent's right foot as shown. Look at how John is using his right forearm to push against Jim's right heel and using his hands to pull in on Jim's upper foot and toes. This creates a nasty ankle twist variation of the toehold.

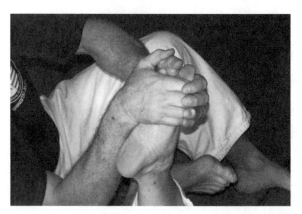

Here's a closer view of this toehold. You can see how both of John's hands are pulling on his opponent's upper foot and toes and John's right wrist and forearm are pushing on the inside of the right heel creating a twisting movement and a lot of pain!

Toehold Against a Head and Arm Hold

Jarrod has Chris in a head and arm hold.

Chris starts his escape by turning his body into Jarrod and kicking his left leg over in an attempt to hook Jarrod's left leg.

As Chris does this with his left leg, Jarrod catches Chris's left leg with his own left leg and foot, stopping Chris's leg hook.

Jarrod uses his left leg to push down on Chris's left leg and Jarrod uses his left hand to grab the top of Chris's left foot.

Jarrod uses his left hand to hook over Chris's left lower leg and ankle and has grabbed his right wrists as shown to form a figure 4 hand hold. Jarrod continues to hold the top of Chris's foot with his left hand and pushes down on Chris's left foot to create the toehold.

The Ankle Crush Toehold

Here's a sneaky little move to use on your opponent when you are riding him. John is riding Chance and has used his right knee to trap Chance's left lower leg and ankle as shown. As he does this, John uses his right hand to reach down and grab Chance's left foot at the toes.

John has used his right knee and lower leg and trapped Chance's left leg. Notice that John's right shin is driving down directly against Chance's Achilles' tendon (which creates a lot of pain) and John is using his right hand to grab and pull Chance's left upper foot at the toes inward. This twisting and crushing action really hurts!

SECTION THREE:
Knee Locks

"I'll go for the knee lock, but even if I don't get it, I still chewed him up on the mat pretty good."
Chris Heckadon, World Sambo Champion

Locking an opponent's knee is one of the most spectacular ways of getting a lower body submission. It usually takes time and real effort to control the position and set your opponent up to sink in the knee lock.

From a tactical point of view, going for a knee lock can be a positive "time waster" in a tight match. Maybe this sounds like stalling (and it pretty much is!) but if you're in a tight match and have a small lead in the score, digging in and leg wrestling with your opponent, then making it all look like you're doing everything possible to get the ankle or knee lock is a great way to convince the referee you're the busier man on the mat and staying active. I've seen it used numerous times in sambo matches and it never fails to impress the referee. If for nothing else, use leglocks and leg wrestling as a tactical tool! However, I'm sure you wouldn't mind at all if, while you're "wasting time" working for a leglock, your opponent taps out from the pressure and pain you've put on him.

There are basically three types of knee locks: the bent knee lock, the knee crank and the straight knee lock (or knee "bar.") One application of the bent knee lock is when you jam a part of your body (or your opponent's body such as his own leg) behind his knee and bend it. Another is anytime you bend your opponent's knee and take it out of its natural range of motion. The straight knee lock takes place anytime you straighten your opponent's knee joint against a fulcrum (such as your crotch, hip or upper leg). Doing this "bars" the knee and causes pressure or pain in the joint. A knee crank occurs anytime you twist of turn the knee outside of its natural range of motion. A knee crank can either be done on a knee that is straight (or mostly straight) or bent.

Bent Knee Lock

There are pretty much two types of bent knee locks. The first is when you jam something on the inside of the knee joint and pull on the leg as Chris is demonstrating on Bob in the photo above. Often, but not always, you pull on your opponent's lower leg and keep it in a straight line with his upper leg. You jam a part of your body inside of your opponent's knee and twist it. The second is shown in the next photo when you bend and twist the knee, causing the leg to go unnaturally out of its range of motion.

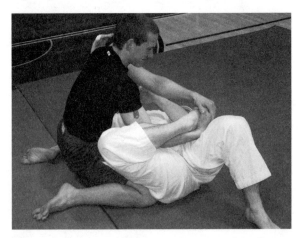

Sometimes the different types of knee locks run together. Above is a bent knee lock and a knee crank. In both cases, you twist or crank your opponent's knee outside of its natural range of motion. Actually, Jarrod has Chris in a double trouble move by twisting his knee and applying a toehold as well!

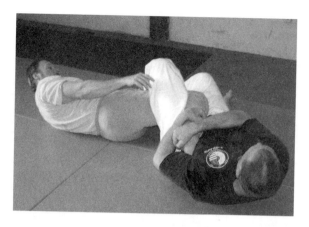

Here's another photo of a knee crank. This one is a subtle, yet very painful knee crank. Often, the knee is cranked as a result of a heel hook, and this application shows this situation. John isolates Steve's upper leg as John rotates Steve's lower leg causing it to twist and crank outside of its natural range of motion. John's left leg is pushing down on Steve's right leg adding to the pressure and making the joint go out of it's natural range of motion.

Straight Knee Lock

Sometimes referred to as a "knee bar" the straight knee lock is a very effective way of producing a tap out. This not only bars the knee joint against a fulcrum (in this case, Kyle is using his hips and crotch as a fulcrum to bar Ben's knee) but it also stretches the entire leg causing muscular pain as well.

STRAIGHT LEGLOCKS

Spin and Stretch Cross-body Knee Lock

This is one of my personal favorites. Bryan has thrown or taken Drew to the mat. Bryan immediately uses his right hand and arm to hook under Drew's right knee. Bryan makes sure to pull Drew's right knee as close as possible to his body as he does this. Also, Bryan quickly bends his knees after throwing Drew to the mat to lower his level so he can be closer to Drew to apply the leglock.

Bryan uses his left knee to jam across and over Drew's right hip as shown here. As he does this, Bryan uses his right arm to pull Drew's knee close to his chest. Bryan now turns to his right, facing Drew's legs and feet.

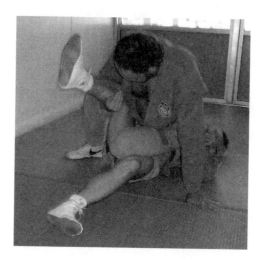

Here's another view of how to jam your knee across the inside of your opponent's near hip. For stability, Steve is using his left hand and arm to post on the mat.

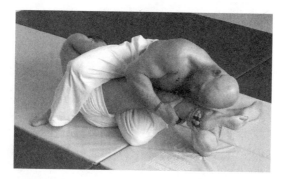

Bryan shoots his left knee hard across Drew's right hip and rolls to his left side as shown in this photo. As he does this, Bryan pulls Drew's right leg in tight to his chest, grabbing it like a baseball bat.

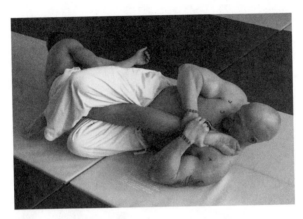

Bryan lands on his left hip and stays in that position so he can exert a lot of pressure when he arches with his hips. As he pulls Drew's right leg in tight to his chest, Bryan arches hard with his hips. Notice how Drew's right knee is jammed in Bryan's crotch. This "bars" Drew's knee and straightens it. Bryan uses both of his legs and feet to hook around Drew's buttocks as he pulls on Drew's right leg.

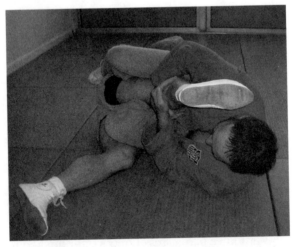

This photo shows a top view of Steve pulling Bill's foot and ankle tightly to his chest and arching his hips into Bill's straightened knee to add more pressure to the knee bar. Look at how Steve has jammed his left knee and shin tightly into Bill's crotch and how Steve has hooks his right leg around and onto Bill's buttocks to make sure there is no space between the bodies and making the leglock tighter and more effective.

Inside to Outside Cross-body Leglock

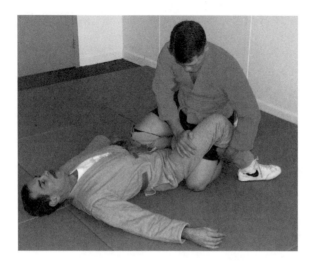

Bob has Chris in his guard, but Chris has pulled back to create distance. Chris then uses his right knee to jam in Bob's crotch. As he does this, Chris uses his left hand to grab Bob's left lower leg.

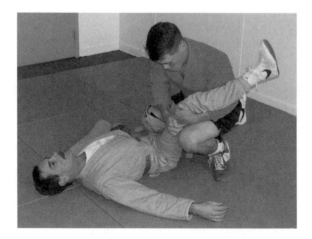

Chris jumps up into a squatting position keeping his right knee jammed in Bob's crotch. Chris makes sure to pinch his knees together to trap Bob's right leg. Chris uses both hands to grab Bob's knee and starts to pull up on it a bit.

Chris quickly slides his right knee across Bob's crotch and right hip and inner thigh and he hugs Bob's right knee to his chest holding on with both hands as shown in this photo.

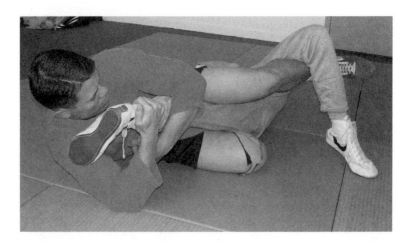

Chris keeps driving his right knee through and lands on his right hip. As he does this, Chris continues to hold onto Bob's leg and pulls it tight to his chest creating a knee bar. Chris pinches his knees together to trap Bob's outstretched right leg and Chris can use his left lower leg and foot to hook into Bob's left knee to help split Bob's legs apart and control them better.

Far Hip Roll to Cross-body Leglock (Opponent is Flat)

This is a good leglock from the top ride position. Kyle is riding Ben, who is flat in the chicken position. Kyle jams his right shin and knee on Ben's left upper leg to trap it. This keeps Ben flat and keeps him from moving away.

Kyle places his right knee on the mat as shown and hooks under Ben's right upper leg with his right hand as shown. Kyle might have to use his left hand to post on the mat for stability.

This is another view of how Kyle has trapped Ben's left leg and hooked under Ben's right upper leg to start the move. Notice how Kyle has his knees wide and hips low for a solid base and has his right foot trapping Ben's left leg immediately above his knee to keep Ben from moving.

Kyle steps over Ben's right hips and upper leg with his left knee as he scoops Ben's upper right leg to his chest as shown in this photo. As Ben rolls to his left, driving his left knee through, he makes sure to pull Ben's right leg to his chest.

Kyle has driven his left knee through and landed on his left hip as shown. As Kyle has rolled onto his left hip, he has continued to pull Ben's leg to his chest and has stretched it out straight. He pinches his legs together, trapping Ben's outstretched right leg. Kyle pulls hard on Ben's lower leg and for extra control, Kyle uses his left arm to hook over Ben's ankle and trap it as shown in this photo.

Kyle has used his left hand to grab behind his head to secure Ben's right leg even more and this photo shows how Kyle has used his crotch as the fulcrum and has barred Ben's right knee. This also stretches the entire leg really hard and hurts more than only the knee.

Cross-body Leglock from Opponent's Leg Scissors

The bottom grappler, Kirt, has managed to trap Chris's right leg in a scissors hold. Chris lessens the control of the scissors on his leg by placing his right foot on the mat and working Kirt's scissor lock as far down Chris's leg as possible, eventually getting it to Chris's lower leg and ankle as shown in this photo. It's important for Chris to have his right foot on the mat as shown for a solid base to work from.

Chris uses his left knee to jam in Kirt's near side (in this case right) ribs and torso. Chris makes sure to really put a lot of pressure on Kirt's torso with his left knee as he pops up and scoops Kirt's left leg with his right arm.

Here's another view of how Chris has jammed his left knee in Kirt's torso and scooped Kirt's left leg. Chris has also posted his right foot on the mat as shown in this photo for better balance and control. Chris has used his right arm to scoop Kirt's left leg and is pulling the leg to his chest.

Chris grabs Kirt's lower leg like he would grip a baseball bat and pulls Kirt's leg to his chest as tightly as possible. As he does this, Chris drives his left knee across Kirt's midsection and then rolls onto his left his with his left knee pointing toward where Kirt's feet were.

As rolls onto his left hip, he hugs Kirt's leg to his chest, arches his hips and applies pressure to Kirt's knee and upper leg. Chris stays on his left side so he can exert more pressure by arching his hips. Kirt's knee is barred across Chris's crotch.

141

Both Leg Breakdown to Straight Knee Lock

This is another one of my favorites and my sambo athletes drill on this move a lot. Steve has moved to the side of Greg who is on all fours. Steve uses both hands to reach through and grab Greg's far knee (in this case, Greg's right knee). Notice that Steve's left hand is down by the knee and his right hand is a bit higher. Make sure not to lace your fingers together.

Steve drives hard into Greg's left (near) hip with his upper chest and body as he uses both hands to scoop Greg's knees and drive Greg onto his right side. Steve has now broken Greg down from a stable to an unstable position.

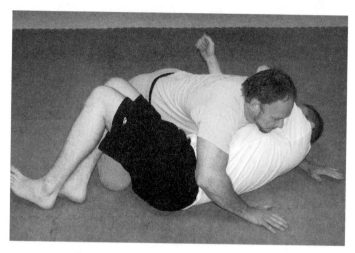

Steve moves up on Greg's body and gets chest-to-chest contact for greater control. Steve is on both knees for stability.

Steve quickly rises up and jams his left lower leg and knee on the top of Greg's torso at the stomach. Steve also makes sure to use his right arm and hand to control Greg's legs. Steve turns to his right as he does this.

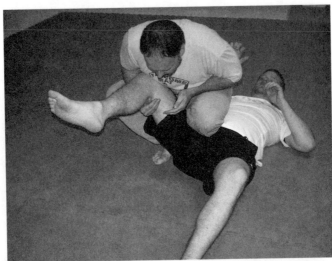

As Steve continues to turn to face Greg's lower body, he continues to slide his left knee down Greg's near (right) hip. As he does this, Steve bends forward and uses both hands to grab Greg's right upper leg and pull it to his chest.

Steve keeps driving forward with his head down and hugs Greg's right leg to his chest. The momentum of Steve driving forward with his left knee jamming between Greg's legs makes Steve's body roll to Steve's left as shown here.

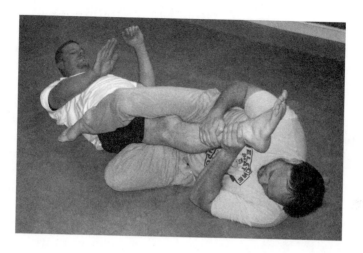

Steve rolls forward and onto his left side as shown. Notice that Steve has pulled Greg's right leg to his chest and is holding it like a baseball bat. Steve is squeezing both of his legs together to trap Greg's right leg. Steve's right leg is hooked over Greg's upper leg and hip.

To create a barring action against Greg's right knee and upper leg, Steve uses his right arm to hook over Greg's right lower leg and uses his right hand to grab his right thigh as shown. Steve arches really hard with both of his hips as he does this.

Rolling Knee Lock (Standing)

This leglock has been around for a long time and is used in sambo frequently. An adaptation where the leg isn't locked is used in judo as well. While it isn't a move that I would recommend you try all the time, it's good to know because you never know when you might surprise an opponent, even a tough opponent, with this rolling leglock. Chris and Steve are facing each other.

Steve uses his left hand to grab Chris's left sleeve (low on the sleeve) and at the same time, uses his right hand to get a high grip on Chris's upper back. This action is called a cross-grip and is really a useful grip for a variety of grappling sports.

Here's another photo of how to cross-grip your opponent with your left hand and take a back grip with your right hand. Will pulls John in close to his body and has excellent control of the situation at this point. Will has pulled John's left hand to his left hip and as he does this, Will closes the space between his body and John's. Notice how close Will's right hip is to John's left hip.

In this photo, Steve is doing the same thing as Will did in the previous photo. Steve has pulled Chris in tight to his body and has Chris's left hand firmly at his left hip and close to his body. Steve is pulling hard with his right hand forward in the direction of Chris's head. As he does this Steve attacks with his right leg and will start a throw on Chris.

As Steve pulls Chris forward with his right hand on Chris's back, he uses his left hand to reach down and grab Chris's left ankle, preferably the ankle. This all takes place as Steve is pulling Chris and rolling him in a forward direction.

Steve does a forward roll over his left shoulder as he pulls Chris hard with his right hand on Chris's back. All the while, Steve holds onto Chris's left ankle with his left hand.

Will is in the middle of his roll on John. This photo shows how Will has a strong grip on the back of John's jacket and is using it to roll John over.

Steve has rolled Chris over and kept control of Chris's left leg and ankle with his left arm. Steve has also made sure to drive his right leg over Chris's left thigh and hip as he maintains control of Chris's left ankle with his left hand. After the roll is completed, Steve will quickly grab Chris's ankle with both hands as if holding a baseball bat and pull back on Chris's left leg.

Steve has grabbed Chris's ankle and is pulling on it as he arches his hips up. Steve is laying on his left hip and side so he can get more power when he arches to lock Chris's knee. Notice that Steve has used his right foot to hook under Chris's right knee, immobilizing it and preventing Chris from rolling into Steve to ease the pain of the leglock or escape.

Will has both of his feet hooked around John's buttocks as he pulls hard on John's left leg and arches his hips to get the leg bar. Will is grabbing John's leg at the ankle like a baseball bat.

To add more pressure to the straight knee lock, Will has hooked over John's left ankle and lower leg with his left arm and wedged John's left foot in his right armpit. This allows Will to arch harder into the action of the leglock.

Here's a back view of how Will has hooked over John's leg and trapped it in his armpit. Notice that Will is on his left hip and not flat on his back so he can drive harder with his hips into the arch and create more pressure to the knee lock.

Rolling Knee Lock (From All Fours)

This is really the same move as done before in the standing version except that the grapplers are not standing. Eric is on all fours and Bret is riding him. Eric makes a point to look around from his position so if Bret posts his left leg (as in the photo) he can take advantage of the situation and grab his leg.

Eric reaches through his legs with his right hand and grabs Bret's leg just above the knee. Eric makes sure to pull it in tight for control.

Eric is grabbing Bret's left leg just above the knee with his right hand as shown in this photo.

As Eric pulls Bret's left leg in tight to his body, he quickly rolls over his right shoulder. As he does this, Eric uses his left leg to whip over in a kicking motion across Bret's left side at the ribs.

153

Eric has completed his right shoulder roll and quickly grabs Bret's left leg with both hands as shown in the photo. Notice that Eric's legs are hooked over Bret's left buttocks.

Eric grabs Bret's left leg with both hands and pulls it tightly to his chest. As he does this, Eric arches hard wit his hips directly into Bret's straightened knee. This creates a knee bar and cause pain in Bret's outstretched knee. Eric makes sure to keep both his feet tightly hooked on Bret's buttocks.

Here's another view of how Eric has applied the knee bar on Bret. It's important to show that Eric isn't laying directly on his back, but rather more on his right hip so he can exert more pressure from the arching action of his hips into Bret's straightened knee.

Straight Knee Lock from the Turk

A big rule when stuck on the bottom is to get your head out and get out of trouble. This method of doing this is called the "Turk" and it is a useful move to get from the bottom position to the top or event lift your opponent up and create a scoring position for yourself. Bret is on the bottom and Eric is riding him from the top.

Bret drives hard into Eric and jams his head in Eric's crotch as shown. As he does this, Bret uses his right hand to grab Eric's left leg above his knee. Bret is using his left hand to post on the mat for stability.

Bret drives into Eric and rises up with his head between Eric's legs as shown. Bret is using his right hand to hold onto Eric's left upper leg and is using his left hand to stabilize Eric's lower left leg.

Bret turns to his right and slams Eric onto the mat onto his back. As he does this, Bret makes sure to move to the outside of Eric's left leg, keeping his head pushed hard on Eric's left inner thigh. Notice that Bret still has control with is right hand on the upper leg and his left hand on the lower leg. Bret is hugging Eric's left upper leg with his right arm, shoulder and head making sure to control it.

Bret steps over Eric's left leg with his right foot and leg and hooks Eric's left leg as shown. Bret continues to hug Eric's right upper leg to him.

Bret now sits through with his with leg and hip and rests on his right hip as shown. Bret uses his left foot to hook Eric's left lower leg and ankle and Bret uses his left leg to really draw Eric's leg back. Bret is using his crotch as the fulcrum and using his left leg to pull Eric's outstretched leg hard. Bret holds on tight with both his hands and arms to continue to trap Eric's upper right leg isolating it and keeping it straight. The pain is in Eric's knee from the knee bar.

BENT LEGLOCKS AND CRANKS

Near Leg Ride Bent Knee Lock

This is a popular leglock from sambo and it's effective. Shawn has Steve in a standing ride and has his left foot forward near Steve's left knee.

Shawn moves to Steve's left side and sinks his left leg in over Steve's left thigh and hip. As he does this, Shawn drives into Steve with his body forcing Steve forward.

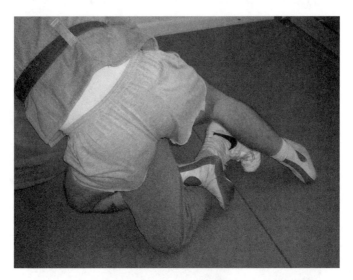

Shawn hooks his left foot over Steve's left lower leg as shown here. Look at how Shawn is using his left foot to trap Steve's left lower leg.

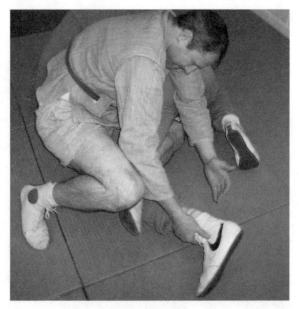

Shawn quickly turns toward Steve's feet and as he does, Shawn uses his left elbow and shoulder to drive into Steve's buttocks. This drives Steve forward. As he does this, Shawn continues to use his left leg and foot to trap Steve's left leg and will use both hands to scoop Steve's left foot an ankle.

Shawn sits (or rolls) back onto his left hip and buttocks, using both hands to pull up on Steve's left foot as shown. Notice how Shawn has jammed his left foot and lower leg slightly sideways in the back of Steve's left knee. By rolling backward, Shawn has driven Steve flat on his front.

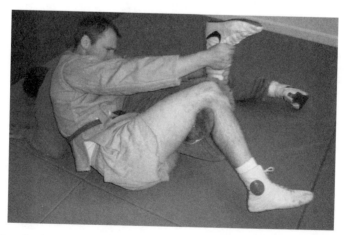

Shawn hooks his right leg over his left foot in a figure 4 position as he continues to pull up on Steve's left foot. To add pressure, Shawn continues to roll backward and uses his left foot to hook down creating more pressure with his figure 4 leglock on Steve's left knee.

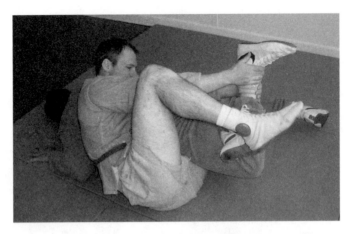

Shawn can also add pressure in another way. If he chooses, Shawn can use his right foot to push down on his left foot. This is a painful application of this leglock and gets a quick tapout!

Near Leg Ride to Bent Knee Lock from the Guard

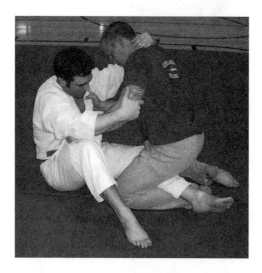

This is a variation of the near leg ride leglock that John Saylor came up with. Chris Bartley (Bartley) is fighting off his buttocks in the guard position and is actually seated on his rear end and not lying flat on his back. He has his left leg between Chris Vanderberg's (Vanderberg) legs as shown.

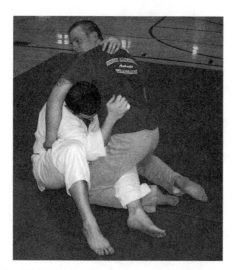

Bartley ducks under Vanderberg's left arm and pulls himself in tight to his opponent.

Bartley reaches forward with his left arm and jams his left elbow against the left hip of Vanderberg. As he does this, Bartley drives his left leg in deeper and starts to pull it to his other foot.

To get his left foot in tight enough, Bartley uses his right hand to grab it and pull it in. this wraps his left leg in deep around Vanderberg's left leg.

Bartley places his right leg over his left foot and may have to use his right hand to help secure it tightly forming a figure 4 position.

Bartley has now formed a good figure 4 (or triangle) with his legs and has used both hands to grab Vanderberg's left ankle. Bartley pulls ups on Vanderberg's left ankle as he rolls backward.

This photo shows a side view of how Bartley has use his legs to figure 4 Vanderberg's left leg and pull up on his foot as he Bartley rolls back to apply pressure to this leglock. Notice that Vanderberg has been flattened out by the action of Bartley rolling back and pulling up on his left ankle.

Outside Knee Jam (Opponent is on All Fours)

Steve is riding Eric from Eric's left side and has his right knee up for mobility. Steve's left knee is on the mat.

Steve quickly turns to face Eric's back end and uses both hands to grab the top of Eric's left foot and pull up on it. As Steve pulls up, he also pulls forward on Eric's foot, away from Eric's body.

Steve pulls hard with both hands on Eric's left foot and collapses Eric flat on his front. To give himself a better pull, Steve jams his left elbow on Eric's buttocks as a lever.

Steve uses his left knee to jam on the back of Eric's left knee as shown. As he does this, Steve uses both hands to pull Eric's left foot up to Steve's chest. Steve's right foot is posted to his side for stability.

Steve drives his left knee hard into the inside of Eric's bent left knee and pulls Eric's left foot to his chest with both hands. Steve leans into Eric's body using the weight of his body to add pressure to the bent knee lock.

Double Leg Knee Jam when Opponent is in the Chicken Position

If your opponent is in the chicken position and crosses his ankles in a defensive manner, this is a good bent knee lock to make him pay for his defensive behavior. Chance is in the chicken position with his ankles crossed and Steve has turned to face Chance's feet.

Steve uses his right arm to scoop under both of Chance's crossed feet and pull them up toward his head. As Steve does this, he posts with his left hand for stability on the far side of Chance's body and uses his left knee to cross over Chance's legs.

Using his right hand, Steve pulls Chances crossed feet to his chest as he jams his left knee into the back of both of Chance's knees. Steve is using his right foot posted wide for stability.

Steve keeps pulling Chance's lower legs and feet to Steve's chest as he starts to lean back toward Chance's hips.

Steve grasps his hands together in a square lock, pulling Chance's feet to his chest and leans back toward Chance's hips and upper body to apply pressure. Steve wants to pull Chance's feet up and toward his chest as he leans back

To add pressure sideways making it a nasty knee crank, Steve leans heavily to his left side and wraps Chance's ankles in his right biceps as shown in this photo. Steve makes sure to squeeze Chance's ankles to Steve's chest as he wraps the ankles in tightly. Steve actually moves his left shoulder back and drives forward with his right hip, making a quick rotation as he cranks Chance's entangled ankles to Chance's left.

Inside Knee Jam (Opponent is on All Fours)

Steve has a wrestler's rid on Chris and has turned to face Chris's back end. Notice that Steve's left hand is hooked over Chris's body for control and Steve is using his right hand to grab the top of Chris's left foot. Steve is pulling Chris' left foot up and away from Chris's body.

Steve has pulled Chris's left foot out and has collapsed Chris onto his front.

Steve quickly moves to his right and toward the back of Chris's left foot and positions himself so he can use his right foot to hook over the top of Chris's left leg as shown. Steve uses his right leg to hook over Chris's left leg directly above Chris's left knee.

Steve uses his right leg to jam in the back of Chris's left knee as shown and uses both hands to grab Chris's belt. Chris' left knee is bent and Steve is leaning hard on Chris's foot and lower leg to add pressure.

Steve uses his hands on Chris's belt to pull himself toward Chris's upper body and lean hard. The combination of Steve's right knee jammed in Chris's left knee and Steve's leaning on it causes pain in Chris's knee.

Knee Jam from A Spinning Cross-body Armlock

Jarrod is attempting an spinning cross-body armlock on Sean.

Sean stands as a defensive move to get away from Jarrod's armlock. As Sean stands, Jarrod shrimps in further to his right getting his head as close as possible to Sean's left foot as possible.

Jarrod uses his right hand to hook around Sean's left leg as shown and as he does, Jarrod pulls his right leg in.

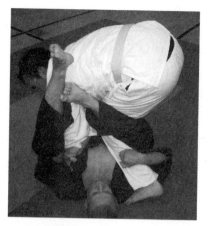

Jarrod uses his right leg to lace around the back of Sean's left knee. Jarrod continues to use his right hand to control Sean's left lower leg. Jarrod will form a figure 4 or triangle with his legs.

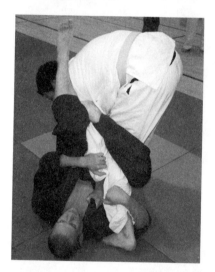

Jarrod's head is still close to Sean's left foot and he is still using his right hand to hold Sean's lower leg. Jarrod laces his legs together in a triangle or figure 4 position around Sean's left leg as shown.

Jarrod uses his right hand to scoop Sean's lower left leg as he uses his legs to push Sean to the mat. Sean will usually fall to his right side as shown. Jarrod keeps a firm triangle hold with his legs on Sean's left leg.

Jarrod quickly uses his left hand to grab Sean's belt (or pants or jacket) and starts to pull himself toward Sean's buttocks. Jarrod's right leg is laced behind Sean's left knee.

Using his arm on Sean's belt, Jarrod pulls himself up maintaining his right leg jammed behind Sean's left knee as shown. As his left knee bends, Sean's left shin and foot are wedged against Jarrod's chest and shoulder.

Jarrod uses his right hand to pull himself up even more toward Sean's upper body as he uses his right knee that is jammed behind Sean's left knee to add pressure to the knee lock. Sean's left lower leg is wedged against Jarrod's chest and right shoulder.

Bent Knee Lock Counter to the Gator Roll

Rusty, on the left, has Travis's right ankle and is attempting to roll to his left to gain momentum with a gator roll. Travis counters by looping his left foot and leg over Rusty's right hip and upper leg. Travis also has control of Rusty's right ankle.

Travis rolls to his buttocks and onto his right hip as Rusty starts his gator roll. Travis uses his left hand to pull Rusty's right ankle and foot toward him and continue to loop his left foot over Rusty's right leg.

Travis sinks his left foot in tight behind Rusty's right knee as Travis continues to pull on Rusty's right foot. Notice that Travis is sitting in his right hip. Travis has to work quickly as Rusty may have enough momentum to secure his ankle lock.

Travis quickly uses his left hand to grab Rusty's jacket, pants or, preferably, belt. Notice how Travis's left arm is on the inside of Rusty's right foot and leg. Travis's left foot is wedged in tight behind Rusty's right knee at this point as Travis rolls even further to his right hip.

To finish the move, Travis grabs with both hands onto Rusty's jacket or belt and pulls himself toward Rusty. The combination of Travis left leg jammed behind Rusty's right knee and Travis pulling himself toward Rusty causes pain in the knee.

Bent Knee Lock Against the Guard

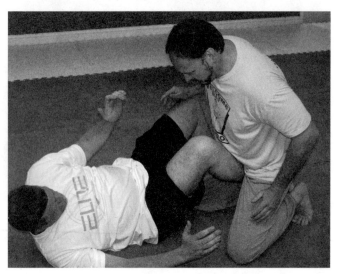

This is an unexpected move by the top grappler in a guard situation. Greg may have jammed his right knee between Steve's legs, or Steve may have moved Greg's right leg between his legs. Either way, Steve wants Greg's right leg between his legs to start the move.

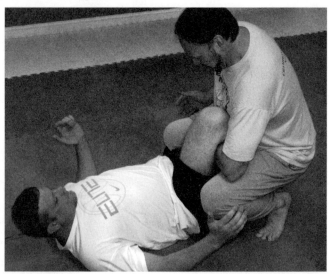

Steve uses his left arm to hook under Greg's right knee as Steve moves in close to Greg to tighten the space between the two bodies. Notice that Steve has squatted and is off his knees at this point. Steve makes sure to use his left arm to pull Greg's right knee as tight as possible to Steve's body.

Steve uses his left hand to grab the top of his left thigh as shown. Doing this cinches Greg's right leg tighter to Steve's body and allows Steve to really use his left forearm to jam under Greg's right knee. Steve is still squatting.

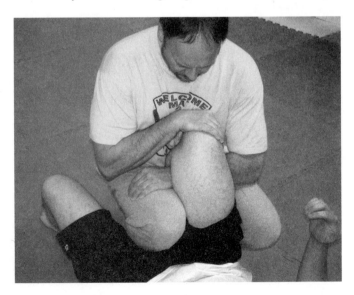

Steve pinches Greg's right leg between his knees as shown and maintains the grip with his left hand on his right thigh. Steve also uses his right hand to grab the top of Greg's knee and pulls Greg's knee in even tighter to Steve's chest. Notice that Steve is still squatting.

Steve sits, or actually rolls, back onto his buttocks as he pulls Greg's right knee with him. The combination of Steve's body rolling back and his left hand jammed under Greg's knee causes extreme pressure on Greg's right knee joint and upper leg.

Bent Knee Crank Counter to Head and Arm Pin

This is a sneaky little move that can surprise your opponent. In fact, the element of surprise is essential for this to work usually. Once your opponent has been caught in it and you are cranking on his knee, it's too late for him. This photo shows John holding Will with a head and arm hold.

Will has moved his legs closer to John to establish a base with his feet on the mat so he can try to bridge out of the pin. John has quickly shifted from lying on his right hip to sitting on his buttocks as shown. As John does this, he reaches back with his left arm and hooks his left hand under Will's right leg at the ankle, and at the same time, he starts to pull Will's right ankle and foot closer to his body, creating an unnatural bend in Will's knee.

John has the option to stay sitting as in the previous photo and pull hard on Will's foot causing the knee crank to take effect. John can also shift back onto his right hip as shown in this photo and pull on Will's right foot. Doing this pulls Will's foot and lower leg more to the outside of his normal range of motion causing severe pain in the right knee and somewhat in the right hip.

Here's a closer view of how John is cranking Will's right knee.

Side Hold to Bent Knee Crank

John has Jim in a side hold and uses his right hand to reach over Jim's body to grab the top of Jim's left foot. As he does this, John pulls it toward Jim's left arm and shoulder. This causes the knee to bend outside of its normal range of motion and is a nasty knee crank. Notice that John has good control of Jim's upper body by hooking under his neck with his left arm.

SECTION FOUR
Hip and Upper Leg Locks

"Splitting a guy apart for a hip lock takes a lot of skill, but it takes a lot of guts to try it first."
Jim Schneweis, U.S. National Sambo Champion and Coach

Some may not classify hip locks as a leg submission, but if you think about it a bit, it does make sense to include it as a leg lock. Even though the primary pain is focused in your opponent's hip, that pain is a result of the unnatural twisting or pulling of the femur from the hip joint. Basically, anytime you stretch or twist your opponent's upper leg and hip, this is classified as a hip or upper leg lock.

Hip locks are dangerous. While the hip is a strong joint, it is possible to dislocate the hip joint with a hip lock.

The three primary hip and upper leg locks are:

1. The **Banana Split** when you split your opponent's legs apart outside of his natural range of motion.

2. The **Grapevine** when you split your opponent's legs wide apart when he is lying either on his front or on his back.

3. The **Crab** when you twist or manipulate your opponent's upper leg, hip and lower back using the weight of your body to add pressure. This is usually done when your opponent is on his front or front side.

Banana Split

Anytime you roll your opponent onto his back or shoulders and stretch his legs apart with your hands and arms, that's a "banana split." Also called the "spladle" this is a painful hold and is used in freestyle and collegiate wrestling as a pin. We use it as a joint lock. However, be careful, as this move can do serious damage to your opponent's hips.

Grapevine

When you lace your legs around your opponent's legs and split them apart, this is a grapevine. Grapevines are used in a variety of holds and can be painful.

The Crab (or Boston Crab)

A "crab" is a painful lower body submission where you control your opponent's leg or legs and turn his over onto his front, then sit on his hips and lean back. This causes considerable pain in the lower back, hips and legs, so be extremely careful when practicing these moves.

HIP LOCKS

The Banana Split (Back Roll)

Bret has secured a near leg ride on Eric with his right leg on Eric's right leg.

Bret leans over Eric's lower back and uses his left hand to hook under Eric's left hip and upper leg. Bret continues to keep his right leg entwined with Eric's right leg.

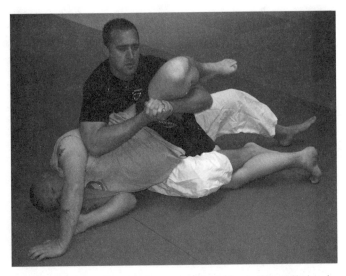

Bret has grabbed his hands together in a square lock. He rolls back onto his buttocks and as he does, he pulls Eric's left leg up and toward him. Notice that Bret still has control of Eric's right leg with his right leg. Bret's left arm is hooked under Eric's left knee.

Bret continues to roll onto his back and as he does, he splits Eric's legs apart by pulling with both hands on Eric's left leg and using his right leg to stretch out Eric's right leg. By rolling back, Bret has rolled Eric back onto his upper back and shoulders.

Bret finishes the move by using his left leg to hook over his right leg and drive down with it, splitting Eric's legs even further apart.

Bret can also use his left foot to drive down on his right lower leg or ankle to split Eric's legs apart.

Rolling Banana Split

The end result is the same as the other banana split application, but his time Bret will roll Eric over onto his back. Bret sinks his right leg in for a near leg ride to set the move up.

Bret reaches over Eric's hips and lower back and uses his left hand to grab Eric's left ankle.

Bret uses his right hand and arm to reach over Eric's left hip. Bret makes sure to grab Eric's left ankle with his right hand. As he does this, Bret makes sure to uses his left hand to pull Eric's lower left leg and foot as close as possible to his left buttocks, bending the left knee as tight as possible.

After Bret makes sure he has bent Eric's left leg as tightly as possible, he does a shoulder roll over his right shoulder. As he rolls, Bret pulls Eric's left foot over with him. Bret still has a strong near leg ride with his right leg on Eric's right leg.

Bret has completed his shoulder roll and has split Eric's legs wide apart.

Here's another view of the finished roll and banana split. Eric's upper back and shoulders are flat on the mat.

Bret uses his left leg to hook over his right leg to form a figure 4 and add more pressure to the banana split. Notice that Bret is pulling hard with both hands on Eric's left leg. Bret's right arm is hugging Eric's left leg and Bret's left hand is controlling Eric's left ankle.

Inside Leg Ride to Banana Split

The banana split usually starts with a near leg ride and this variation is no exception. Steve has secured a near leg ride with his left leg on Chance's left leg.

This is pretty much the same move as the first banana split shown, but the big difference in this move is how Steve traps Chance's far (right) leg with both of his hands before he starts his roll. Steve has used his left hand to reach under Chance's body and hook Chance's right shin (palm up). Steve has used his right hand to grab (palm down) Chance's right ankle. As he does this, Steve pulls up on Chance's right leg and traps it against Chance's right buttocks as shown. He also starts to roll back toward his left hip.

Steve rolls back onto his left hip and onto his back. As he does this, he uses both hands to pull Chance's right bent leg to his chest and uses his left leg to split Chance apart.

Here's another view of how Steve has rolled onto his back and has hooked his right leg over Chance's left leg to add pressure to Chance's left leg and is hugging Chance's right leg to Steve's chest.

Steve can also use a figure 4 leg position to split Chance's legs apart.

UPPER LEG AND JOINT LOCKS

The Grapevine from the Vertical Hold (Mount)

When you wrap your legs around your opponent's legs as shown here, this is a "grapevine." Usually, grapevines take place in one of two positions. The first is shown here as Steve is holding Shawn in a vertical hold and has split Shawn's legs wide apart with a grapevine. It's important for Steve to not only split Shawn's legs wide, but also to arch with his hips to add more pressure to the move. Even if your opponent doesn't tap out from the stretching of his legs. You have him in a secure hold using good leg wrestling to maintain your hold-down.

The Grapevine from the Rodeo Ride

You can often apply more pressure with a grapevine from the rodeo ride position than from the top position because you can arch harder with your hips and rock forward which forces the bottom man's lower body to rise up as shown here. Eric has John in a rodeo ride and has flattened him out and grapevined his legs.

Here's a back view of how Eric has grapevined John's legs and is arching with his hips and rocking forward to add pressure to the hold. Even if you don't get the tap out from the grapevine, you have a great rodeo ride and can work for a choke or other move from this position.

Boston Crab (1 Leg) from an Ankle Pick

This is an old move that has a lot of history to it. This is a favorite legit pro wrestlings move that has been around for many years. Will has taken Bret to the mat and has hooked his right arm under Bret's left lower leg and used his left hand to grab Bret's left shin. Will forms a figure 4 hold with his hands by using his right hand to grab his left wrist. Will makes sure to have the top of Bret's left foot wedged in tight behind his right armpit. As he does this, Will starts to pull up on Bret's left leg and uses his left leg to step in close to Bret's body between his legs.

Will uses his right leg to step over Bret's left hip turning Bret over onto his front as shown. Will keeps a firm hold on Bret's left ankle.

Will has stepped over Bret with his right leg and has Bret mostly (if not completely) flat on his front. To apply pressure, Will arches forward with his hips and straightens his body. This causes a lot of pain in Bret's hips and entire left leg and especially in Bret's lower back.

Boston Crab (2 Legs) Against the Guard

Bret has Will in his guard, but Will starts to back away to make space between the two bodies.

Will uses his right hand to scoop under Bret's left knee as shown as he starts to stand with his left foot.

Will stands up and makes sure to keep Bret's upper body pinned to the mat, even briefly, but keep it pinned there as long as Will needs to so he can control Bret's legs and hips better.

Will has grabbed Bret's right knee with his left hand and uses his right hand, which is firmly holding Bret's left knee, to start to turn Bret over. Will uses his right leg to start to step over Bret's left hip and side to turn Bret over.

Will has turned Bret over flat onto his front and has kept a firm grip with both hands on both of Bret's knees. Will makes sure to pull Bret's knees and legs up and toward Will's' upper body for more control. As he does this, Will starts to straighten his body, arch his hips forward and lean back to cause pain in Bret's legs and especially in the lower back.

Will may choose to let go of one of Bret's legs to concentrate on a single leg hold. In this photo, will maintains control of Bret's right leg with his left arm and lets go of Bret's left leg.

Will grabs his hand together in a square lock and sits back on Bret's buttocks and lower back. Will is careful to do this slowly to avoid a dangerous situation for Bret. Do not sit back quickly and with great force, as this will cause permanent injury to your opponent.

ABOUT THE AUTHOR

Steve Scott holds advanced black belt rank in Kodokan Judo and Shingitai Jujitsu and is a member of the U.S. Sombo Association's Hall of Fame. He started his career in judo and jujitsu in 1965 in Kansas City, Missouri and was introduced to sambo in 1976. As an athlete, he won several medals in the National AAU Sambo Championships, including gold twice. He also was an active athlete in the sport of judo and competed in regional and national judo events (as well as sambo events) from 1965 through 1987. As a coach, he has developed over 150 national champions in the sports of judo, sambo, sport jujitsu and submission grappling at his Welcome Mat Judo, Jujitsu and Sambo Club in Kansas City, Missouri. Steve has trained, competed and coached in North America, South America, Europe and Japan.

Steve served as the National (Under 21) Coach and Development Director, as well as the Coach Education Director for United States Judo, Inc., the official governing body for judo recognized by the U.S. Olympic Committee in the United States in the late 1980s through the early 1990s. He also served as the Chairman of the National AAU Judo Committee and is currently active in the AAU judo and jujitsu national programs. Steve has also served as the coach for official U.S. teams for both judo and sambo in many international competitions, including the Pan American Games, World Judo (Under 21) Championships and World Sambo Championships as well as the annual Pan American Judo Championships, International High School Judo Championships and many other international judo and sambo events. Steve has also coached champions at the Arnold Classic Submission Grappling Championships and numerous champions in sport jujitsu national events.

Steve is also the television color analyst for the Titan Fighting Championships based in Kansas City, Missouri and conducts seminars and clinics in submission grappling for MMA fighters. He has authored several books including COACHING ON THE MAT, SECRETS OF THE CROSS-BODY ARMLOCK, CHAMPIONSHIP SAMBO, ARMLOCK ENYCLOPEDIA, THE GRAPPLER'S BOOK OF STRANGLES AND CHOKES and THE MARTIAL ARTS TERMINOLOGY HANDBOOK. He has also authored numerous technical articles for a variety of judo magazines and is featured in Turtle Press' DVD CHAMPIONSHIP SAMBO. Steve is available for seminars and clinics and can be reached through his web page at www.WelcomeMatJudoClub.com.

Index

Also Available from Turtle Press:

Boxing: Advanced Tactics and Strategies
Grappler's Guide to Strangles and Chokes
Fighter's Fact Book 2
The Armlock Encyclopedia
Championship Sambo
Complete Taekwondo Poomse
Martial Arts Injury Care and Prevention
Timing for Martial Arts
Strength and Power Training
Complete Kickboxing
Ultimate Flexibility
Boxing: A 12 Week Course
The Fighter's Body: An Owner's Manual
The Science of Takedowns, Throws and Grappling for Self-defense
Fighting Science
Martial Arts Instructor's Desk Reference
Solo Training
Solo Training 2
Fighter's Fact Book
Conceptual Self-defense
Martial Arts After 40
Warrior Speed
The Martial Arts Training Diary for Kids
Teaching Martial Arts
Combat Strategy
The Art of Harmony
Total MindBody Training
1,001 Ways to Motivate Yourself and Others
Ultimate Fitness through Martial Arts
Taekwondo Kyorugi: Olympic Style Sparring

For more information:
Turtle Press
1-800-77-TURTL
e-mail: orders@turtlepress.com

http://www.turtlepress.com